Beyond the Rivers of Ethiopia

Dr. Mensa Otabil

PNEUMA LIFE

PUBLISHING

Beyond the Rivers of Ethiopia

by Dr. Mensa Otabil

Published by:

PUBLISHING

Printed in the United States of America

ISBN 1-56229-404-0

Pneuma Life Publishing
P.O. Box 10612
Bakersfield, CA 93389
(805) 837-2113

CONTENTS

ACKNOWLEDGMENTS

My Love and Appreciation to my wife Joy for being a helpful partner and friend.

To my friends in the Ministry, William Obeng Darko, Eric Kwapong, Bob Hawkson, Peter Morgan, Bertril Baird, Kingsley Fletcher, Myles Munroe, Edwin Donkor, Michael Essel, Nii Tackie Yarboi and Andrew Wutawunashe for their suggestions and encouragement to produce this book.

To Miss Patricia Brown, Cephas Narh and T. Sowah who prepared the manuscript for printing.

Above all, to God Almighty for His gift of Wisdom to me.

DEDICATION

To my three little children - **Sompa, Nhyira, Yoofi** and their friends - Nyamekye, Nana Siaw, Tabua, Maame Anamua, Papa Obeng, Nana Ama, Kiaski, Ziona, Awura Adjoa, Paa Kojo, Aseda, Anyidado, Abayie, Awura Ama, Mansa, Ewura Ekua, Kwamina, Louisa, Alice, Kwame, Bebee, Myma, Papi, Judah, Paa Kofi, Panyin, Kakra, David, Zoe, Lady Asaph, Roberta, Adolph, Sarah, Yooku, Maame Henewa, Brother, Nii Soosi, Nii Dromo, Nhyira, Nana Nkansah, Maame Nkansah, Naju, Nana Boakye, Hedzoleh, Sharon, Nii Abo, Kobby, Kuuku, Afriyie, Joojo, Ama, Josephine, Nana Yaa, Pamela, Akos, Samoa, Naa Odole, Naa Dzama, Naa Ayorkor, Nii Odoi, Mother, Mickey, Yvonne, Odomfonoba, Dorcas, Egyiir, Akosua, Amoba, Naa Asheley, Naa Oode, Nana Osae, Nana Boafo, Dzinpa, Rejoice, Julia, Amakour, Makafui, Queenster, Franklin, Paula, Miimi, Ayeyi, Nelly, Owusuaa, Gracious, Claribel, Paa Kwesi, Abenaa, Enyonam, Hossana, Caleb, Edem, Lauretta, Eyram, Abena Konadu, Goodman, ObengDarko, Natasha, Naa Amoah, Arabella, Nyamenaose, Bombi, Nooni, Borgie, Paul, Anna-Kissel, Damaris Joy ...

May Your Generation be totally free to fulfill God's Purpose.

FOREWORD

As an African-American child growing up in Pompano Beach, Florida in the 1950's and 1960's, I was constantly and yet painfully reminded of my place and identity in a small, segregated southern town. The railroad track was the dividing line between two separate and unequal societies - one white and one black, with well defined boundaries characterized by racism. My parents often admonished us to be careful in addressing white folks, to always say "Sir."

As a lad, I watched our Christian neighbor beaten to the ground with a baseball bat, by "goons," who were under orders of a racist farmer because he refused to farm. I saw persons dehumanized, families destroyed, and communities divided by negative principalities and powers generated by the "Man." I remember the economic bondage engendered by a sharecropping system that forever kept us in debt. We were taken from school in order to harvest crops. When African-Americans murdered other African-Americans, they more often than not were freed before the week had past. The cumulative effect of these day-to-day experiences created serious identity crises for African-Americans in my time.

Added to this was the presentation of a blonde, blue-eyed, Europeanised Christ, the product of an artist's imagination. We tried to trust this Christ, but way down in our hearts, something was lacking. Once we discovered the manly Christ of scripture, we became uncomfortable with a Euro-centric Christ that did not square with our manhood. We longed for a Christ who could break the bonds of oppression and set the captives free. We longed for a God who would keep His word, regardless of what it took. A God who was bound to His people by covenant.

For too long, racially biased teachings on the role of Blacks in the Bible have been obscured by European and Euro-American biblical scholars. They have either omitted or treated lightly those areas that mention a Black presence in scripture. Thanks to God, the European, Euro-American dominance on biblical scholarship has been broken, and God is using the offspring of those who did not participate in the African Diaspora.

The new conversations and new listening posts are now derived from developing nations from the southern hemisphere, rather than the more affluent, highly industrialized nations of the North. Biblical conversation is now developing from those persons who have been labelled the "wretched of the earth." This new example may also signal the strong admonition of scripture that the "last shall be first and the first shall be last." (Matthew 20:16)

The moment of truth is upon us. Time, pregnant with meaning, now dogs our footsteps. The tables have been turned, America needs to be evangelized. Our inner cities have been labelled urban war zones, characterized by urban, guerrilla warfare. The evangelization process has begun. The Black religious experience extends far beyond the boundaries of the African-American religious experience. It is inclusive of those persons whose birth, self-understanding, and world-view fall within the African race. At the forefront of this reverse thrust to save America is **Pastor Mensa Otabil** of Accra, Ghana.

At the heart of this book is a challenge and call to the offspring of the children of the African Diaspora, and those who remain, to come to grips with our true identity. The pages that follow do not present simplistic, unfounded rambling through the maze of scripture with no sound footing. While it is not a technical, exegetical work, scholarship comes through. It is written for those who are willing to listen with head and heart. It is difficult to read this work and not become involved as a participant.

I applaud one who is willing to stand in our historic homeland and track the biblical narrative in a new way, as he lifts up such blatant omissions as Keturah's six children, fathered by Abraham. They were "given gifts and sent East." These were the black children of Abraham who lost their inheritance legally, according to Dr. Otabil.

The Midianites were the children of Abraham by Keturah. Moses sat at the feet of the priest of Midian, and married Zipporah. For Dr. Otabil, racism is an old problem. It surfaced when Moses' marriage to an Ethiopian became an issue. His insistence on having a sense of history is invaluable. He explodes long-held myths about Africa, and exhorts us to unite. With clarity of vision and voice, Mensa beckons us toward God's new future.

We must go "beyond" in order to go forward. To follow Dr. Otabil's conversation is to embrace a new badge of identification, even if we have to go beyond the rivers of Ethiopia to rediscover it.

Leonard Lovett, PhD.
Oral Roberts University
Tulsa, Oklahoma

1

UNDERSTANDING

When I was a little boy, I heard this story about how God created the different races of the world. It is said that at the time of the creation of mankind, God Almighty had a big pond into which He threw His creation.

The first beings to be thrown into the pond were fully submerged in the water of the pond and as such, came out totally washed, cleansed and lily-white.

The second batch did not turn out very white but came out a bit yellowish.

The third batch got in when the water in the pond was quite depleted and muddied so they came out brownish-red and by the time the last batch had their turn they could only touch the water with the soles of their feet and their palms, so they came out very dark on their body with only the soles of their feet and their palms partially cleansed.

Well, you can guess who came out lily-white and who only got their palms and soles cleansed! I don't know how that story gained popularity, but I can remember that amongst us kids, at least in my neighborhood, it was somehow our standard explanation for the differences between the races.

The essence of that myth was to create racial superiority for one group and inferiority for another. It made one group appear as God's first choice and another as beneficiaries of the leftover of humanity. When people distort history, they can easily isolate you in order to dominate you.

The spirit of racism thrives on misinformation and stereotyping. Instead of portraying people in the likeness of God, it seeks to devalue the worth of people who are different from us as not being as good as we are. Just because somebody does not talk the way you talk, dress the way you dress and look the way you look, does not in any way imply that they are inferior or superior to you. Different does not mean better.

See, Hear, Understand and Know

Job said in Chapter 13 verses 1 and 2 of his book:

> **"Lo, mine eye hath seen all this, mine ear hath heard and understood it, What ye know, the same do I know also; I am not inferior unto you."**

That is an awesome statement! Inferiority is developed when you do not see what someone else sees, hear what he hears, understand what he understands or know what he knows. So then if any individual or group of people meant to dominate you, they would endeavor to manipulate what you see, hear and understand.

That has been the method used by all oppressive human institutions, be their governments, religious organizations or corporations. That is why the media represents the most potent force for either the control or the liberation of a people. When someone controls what you see, hear, understand and know, he can make you feel inferior about yourself and develop a sense of self-hatred and alienation.

The world's power structures perpetuate themselves through a meticulous and systematic network, designed to keep their subjects in total ignorance. Even in the church world, until the Great Reformation of the 16th Century, the Word of God remained chained and unavailable to the body of Believers. The entrance of God's word into an individual brings to that one the light of liberation and thereby frees the individual. A free man can never be bound.

In 1832, the U.S. Senator Henry Berry made this often quoted, revealing statement to the Virginia House of delegates, concerning the state of the Negro slaves, he said:

"We have as far as possible, closed every avenue by which light may enter the slave's mind. If we could extinguish the capacity to see the light, our work would be complete. They would then be on the level with the beast of the field and we should be safe."

Senator Berry died a long time ago but the structures his generation put into place to further their agenda, are still being used to keep our people from being enlightened. Friend, this statement was not an isolated one but a fair representation of the logic of the powers that be in that era. It still is the logic of this era!

The images we see on the TV screens are constantly influencing our attitudes either for good or for evil. As a black man, I have observed this war being waged from all fronts to portray our people in a very negative light.

Several years ago, I watched the movie, "The Wild Geese" which dramatized a mercenary maneuver to liberate an imprisoned ex-president from a fictionalized African State. Being one to admire precise execution of military operations, the movie naturally had my full emotional attention when I was viewing it. From the beginning of the movie, you are made to identify with the mission of the mercenaries.

Your sympathies would be for those European-trained commandos, who were depicted as the heroes in their efforts to out-smart the hordes of African "natives," who were the villains.

Surprisingly, during the time I was viewing the movie, I never stopped to think that the commandos were just paid soldiers of fortune doing the dirty job for a ruthless, multi-national investor, whose only interest in the whole operation was his money. Several times during the screening of the movie, I found myself hoping for the foreign intruders to decimate the sons of the soil.

Later on, in reflection, I did a mental playback of events in some of the scenes in the movie and realized how the tools of manipulation had been employed to make me hate my own. I enthusiastically watched the European butcher, the African and actually felt saddened when one of the "heroes" died just before the commando airplane took off.

To me, these sentiments reflect the brutal effects of self-negation and alienation that has plagued Africans and people of African descent over the years. As liberated as I thought I was, the effect of that movie brought into sharp focus the subtle and subliminal attempt to condition my mind to accept as normal the supremacy of one race over another.

These same methods are used to reconstruct and change historical facts to smooth over the mistakes of one people against another, as had been done through the cowboy and Indian movies. Somehow, I think as children we have innocently imbibed images and concepts which have together made us vulnerable to foreign control and domination.

The average black person will, for almost all his life, read books which were not written by his people. He will watch films that portray another race as the heroes. His children will play with "white" dolls which then become the standard of beauty, and watch cartoon scenes that are not relevant to his identity. Even our Bible Colleges have little or no materials written by our own people.

What we see, hear, understand and know has been so tightly controlled that when you grow up, you could spend all your life unconsciously trying to be like somebody else. With this condition, why would you not feel inferior about yourself!

The Truth Liberates

To counteract this negative situation, the words of Jesus Christ in John 8:32 prove very valuable. In a sense it re-echoes the words of Job. Jesus said:

"And ye shall know the truth, and the truth shall make you free."

The opposite of Jesus' words are also true; *"You shall know the lie and the lie will keep you in bondage."*

You cannot effectively battle lies with lies. That simply compounds the bondage. The Truth experienced and known is the key to the total liberation of any oppressed people.

Jesus did not say that knowing the Bible will set you free, because a lot of misinformation has been fed into the world through a misrepresentation of the Bible's total revelation.

Just memorizing and quoting Bible verses will not set anyone free. Knowing the Bible does not necessarily mean you know the truth! Jesus also did not say: "You shall know religion and religion shall set you free" because much of what religion does is keep people under bondage. That is why Jesus always had problems with the Pharisees and the religious leaders of His time. He did not bring us a "religion", He brought us the liberating truth about God and man!

Many of us Christians have been religiously brainwashed. So much so that we are bound by what our religious denomination says instead of what the Spirit of Truth is revealing. I think the Muslims are worse off in this regard. They give their converts Arabic names and let them pray in Arabic, facing an Arabic land!

It is amazing that in this modern 20th Century, there are still people who persist in believing that Africa is Tarzan's jungle domain with people living in trees and fighting lions and elephants. That is how the world's misinformation apparatus has portrayed a part of God's people.

African-Americans have been led to believe that their motherland is a jungle and that slavery was a favor done them because it brought them into civilization. Sad to say, many have bought into that lie.

If this stereotyped image is portrayed to anyone who does not really know the truth, it creates a negative response in that individual.

On the other hand, some parts of the world are portrayed as the ultimate in human comfort and pleasure until you discover the truth about the rape, murder and destitution in those societies. In this case, both the deceiver and the deceived become captives in their own little isolated corners. It is only the truth that will set us free, to be what God wants us to be.

I strongly believe that God is sovereignly changing the times and seasons of the world to bring about a visitation of His power through the Spirit of Truth. His first stop will be the Church, because judgement begins in the house of God.

2

GOD'S VISITATION

Whenever God comes to town He visits the oppressed to set them free. When He visited Moses He said: "Go and tell Pharaoh; Let my people go." The Pharaohic systems of this world must get ready to hear God say again: "Let my people go." Psalm 146:5-7

Happy is he that hath the God of Jacob for his help, whose hope is in the Lord his God:

Which made heaven and earth, the sea, and all that therein is: *Which keepeth truth forever:*

Which executeth judgment for the oppressed: which giveth food to the hungry. *The Lord looseth the prisoners.*

All over the world, there is the feeling that God is once more shaking the nations. Kingdoms are falling and people who had for years been bound through misinformation, by oppressive political systems, are experiencing liberty. The mighty pillars of Apartheid are crumbling before our eyes and the prisoners are coming out free. It is as if a divine clock is ticking to signify a new time for the nations of the world. God is visiting the nations of the world and sovereignly overthrowing powers and domains. He is setting the oppressed free by allowing a new wind of truth to blow across the land.

I believe what we are seeing is the beginning of more fundamental and foundational changes. There is a shaking in the land! God is going to visit the black people of this world to bring them out of the state they are in, into their portion. As I travel to the Caribbean, the United States, Europe and Africa, there is a sense of urgency and a feeling of an appointment with destiny among black people. It is a feeling that makes you know that your time has come, and God is bringing to fruition the days of intense intercessions for His justice to prevail.

I keep running into preachers declaring this message of restoration for the black race. It sometimes makes non-black people nervous to hear their black brothers preach this message. As a matter of fact, there is nothing to be nervous about because God is not destroying one race to lift up another. All He is doing is bringing the truth that would destroy the oppressive and discriminatory structures in the church and the world, so as to establish His purposes for the nations.

The church world is going to have some major shakings as the truth of God marches on. It is a shame to know the pillars of apartheid were built on the teachings of the Dutch Reformed Church. I have actually read a book written by a "Bible-believing"

Canadian Minister which taught that the black man is what the Bible calls the "beast of the field." This teaching would have been funny if it was not so pathetic and destructive!

Anti-Oppression Serum

Because of the role organized religion has played in the domination of the black race, there is the cry in many quarters for us to go back to our ancestral religions and totally reject the Bible. That is not the way out! When a man is bitten by a snake, it takes an anti-snake bite serum prepared from a snake to bring healing and restoration to that person. I totally believe that if the Bible was misused and misapplied to bind our people, we would need an Anti-Oppression Serum prepared from the revealed Truth in God's word to bring healing, liberty and restoration to us.

In the Book of Numbers Chapter 21, the people of Israel suffered a plague of snakes as a result of their murmuring. This killed a lot of people and threatened the survival of the whole nation until the people sought the face of God in forgiveness and asked for a remedy.

Therefore the people came to Moses, and said, We have sinned, for we have spoken against the LORD, and against thee; pray unto the LORD, that he take away the serpents from us. And Moses prayed for the people.

And the LORD said unto Moses, Make thee a fiery serpent, and set it upon a pole: and it shall come to pass, that every one that is bitten, when he looketh upon it, shall live.

And Moses made a serpent of brass, and put it upon a pole, and it came to pass, that if a serpent had bitten any man, when he beheld the serpent of brass, he lived.

As we look again into the Word of God, let the truth in His word about us as a people restore the broken confidence and dignity.

It is only then that you can look at all the negatives committed against you and see that it is only a form which has no effect on you. The Word of God takes the sting from the bite.

Anger does not liberate, it makes you a victim instead of a victor! It is only the truth which will set you free. The Word of God is the key to Freedom!

Preachers from Africa and of African descent can no longer continue preaching an escapist, pie-in-the-sky message. We cannot continue singing about the "flying away" message, while our people battle the harsh realities of life. I fully believe in heaven and hell; but I also believe that God created man on earth to have dominion and not to be dominated by poverty, ignorance and fear.

We need to re-define our theology to establish the true liberty of Christ in the lives of our people. They must know the truth!

Take The Veil Off

2 Corinthians 3:12-14 states:

Seeing then that we have such hope, we use great plainness of speech.

And not as Moses, which put a veil over his face, that the children of Israel could not steadfastly look to the end of that which is abolished:

But their minds were blinded: for until this day remaineth the same veil untaken away in the reading of the old testament; which veil is done away in Christ.

Just as Moses covered his face with a veil, many of us read the Bible with blindfolds on.

In my early Christian life, nobody ever taught me that black people played any role in the Bible. It was as if a veil covered my eyes whenever I read the Bible, because I assumed that all the characters in the Bible were white. I used to wonder about how come my people were deprived and oppressed on every continent that they lived.

Our treasures were misused and our people abused long before we were born. Our generation just inherited the fruits of colonialism and slavery. There must be an explanation why a whole race could be so dominated.

The African primal religion, which seeks to understand God through His creation developed a philosophy that explains away the inexplicable, as a manifestation of deity. God, then is not a far removed being in heaven, but lives among men and works through the agency of lesser gods who sometimes inhabit trees, rivers, mountains and even manifest themselves in human apparitions. This has led to the revering and in many instances the worship of the creature instead of the Creator.

It is easy in my mind to imagine how the first Africans might have felt on first seeing this individual that had a pale skin, long hair, blue eyes and spoke a different language, with the ability to work "miracles" through his technological advancement. The logical option for those early Africans was to reason out the situation the only way they knew how; and that was spiritual. This human apparition was either a demon or a messenger from the gods. I guess they decided on the latter. For any adventurous explorer in those days, whether he was a trader or a missionary, this situation would be the most heaven-sent opportunity to exploit.

The first missionaries introduced their African converts to their religion and their "God." This deity had long blond hair, long beard, blue eyes and had a pale complexion. In effect, the image which the missionary presented to the African looked just like the missionary! Whoever tried to portray Jesus Christ as an Anglo-Saxon might have had very noble reasons to help his people identify with Christ.

However, for other racial groupings, I think without helping the people to know Christ on a personal basis it amounts to cultural-imperialism to just present

Him as an image. The logic that this situation produces is that if the missionary's race looks just like his 'God' then they were in one class and the rest of us in another class.

It is little wonder that in Ghana, we have a saying which literally translated means; "When you see the white man you have seen your God." That is a total blasphemy and an abomination! It is supplanting the image of God with the image of man.

In order to change that concept, black people have advocated that Jesus Christ should be portrayed as a black man. That is swinging from one extreme to another. Their frustration is real but the answer is wrong.

2 Corinthians 5:16 has this to say:

"Wherefore henceforth know we no man after the flesh: yea, though we have known Christ after the flesh, yet now henceforth know we him no more."

In other words, although Jesus Christ was manifested among men in a physical form, you can only know Him through the Spirit. The physical image of the man Jesus therefore is of no consequence in your knowledge of Him. He is beyond our petty color-barriers and transcends race.

It tickles me to see people hang in their homes plaques with the inscription, "Christ is the Head of this House.. " and then have an image of a Scandinavian- looking man represented who they say is Jesus.

If that was Jesus, what about the other picture in the other room which portrays a man that looks German! Let's take the veil off our eyes and really know Him in Spirit and in truth.

A New Nature Not a Foreign Culture

Because the early missionaries did not understand us, they assumed that everything about us was evil and demonized. Our names were all thought to be demonized, our songs and music forms and even clothing were seen as evil. In their place, we were *christened* with new European names, put on European clothing and sung musical forms that did not move us. All this the missionaries did, forgetting that some of the celebrations they presented as Christian and some of the music forms which were accepted as church music used to be employed in pagan rituals and sung in the taverns. You see, musically, there is no pagan "B flat," worldly "B flat," and Christian "B flat." B flat is B flat! Music forms are not evil in themselves, it is the musician and the lyrics that may be evil. Instead of introducing us to the new nature in Christ, we were introduced to a new culture from Europe!

Christianity came to us clothed with European cultural norms, so much so that it becomes difficult to separate the wheat from the chaff.

Much of what is seen as Christianity is just chaff! Rituals, ceremonies, celebrations, legalism and ignorance. For most people, Christianity was and still is just an external status symbol because when crisis hits, they regress to the power of the fetish. Just wearing a shirt and a tie and having a nice English name will not drive out demons until you have had a personal encounter with the Lord Jesus, which makes you really know that He is relevant, Yesterday, Today and Forever. The Gospel must be proclaimed in power and simplicity.

Paul said in Romans 1:16

"For I am not ashamed of the Gospel of Christ: for it is the power of God unto salvation..."

The power of God is in the Gospel and not a picture or symbol.

The Gospel outlines God's plan of salvation that whosoever, black, white, yellow, red - believes will have eternal life. When the Bible talks about eternal life, the reference is not just to a futuristic promise, but to a dynamic relationship with God that literally affects every aspect of life here on earth. The Gospel does not just emphasize the teachings of Jesus, it reveals God's forgiveness through the eternal atonement of the shed blood of Christ. It is God's response to man's universal need for atonement, cleansing and restoration of relationship.

When the Gospel is presented in truth, it focuses your faith not in Jesus the Jew, but in Christ the Son of the Living God. The Gospel exalts the believer with the gift of righteousness. It brings value and honor to the believer. Knowing the story of Christ and His teachings without having a personal relationship with Him, is like knowing all about the sweetness of a pudding but not having experienced its taste. Biblical Christianity is not a cultural introduction but the experience of a new nature.

2 Corinthians 5:17:

> **"Therefore, if any man be in Christ, he is a new creature: old things are passed away; behold, all things are become new."**

I received Christ as Lord without fully grasping the depth of my experience. My salvation did not radically change my earlier mental programming; I sort of got saved without being converted. Salvation is of the Spirit, but conversion takes place when an individual's mind has been effectively renewed to conform to the Spirit of Christ.

As I grew in the knowledge of Christ, I became more and more acquainted with His truth and consequently started questioning things I had always taken for granted. From then on something inside of me would rise up in rebellion against any suggestion that I was intrinsically inferior to another because of my heritage and the pigmentation of my skin. I took steps to reclaim that which was lost.

I have had people come up to me and ask,

"Is Mensa Otabil your full name?"

I reply "Well my full name is Mensa Anamua Otabil."

"You mean you don't have any Christian name."

"Oh sure I do" I would respond, "Mensa is my Christian name."

"You mean you don't have a name like John, Daniel, Charles,?"

I tell them, "John is the Greek version of a Hebrew name and some of the names you have in mind may be English, French, German or Portuguese."

You see, no name by itself is Christian because Christianity is not about names but a relationship with Christ. It is a Christian person who makes a name Christian, and not the other way round. If I am a Christian, whatever name I bear is Christian!

We also have people who refer to certain places here on earth as "Holy Land." Well, the Bible teaches under the New Testament that wherever two or three are gathered in the name of Jesus Christ they can be assured of God's presence.

Answering the question of the woman of Samaria, Jesus said:

> **Woman, believe me, the hour cometh, when ye shall neither in this mountain, nor yet at Jerusalem worship the father... But the hour cometh, and now is, when the true worshippers shall worship the Father in Spirit and in truth; for the Father seeketh such to worship Him.**
> John 4:21-23

With such understanding of what Christianity is about, I have desired to help break the imposed bondage that man's religion has put on my kinsmen according to the flesh.

Later, when I was called into ministry, one of the things the Lord led me to do was to liberate my people from mental slavery through the preaching of the Gospel, and to lift up the image of the black man so as to be a channel of blessing to the nations of the world. The Scriptures opened up to me in a new way and revealed to me things I had never been taught as a Christian. One of the questions that had agitated my mind was whether black people had played any role in the Bible. Did God ever use Black People? Are we on God's Agenda?

3

Abraham
Father of Many Nations

God's call to Abraham stands out in the Scriptures as the beginning of a new revelation of Himself to man. Over the years, before this call, the nations of the world had descended into a state of apostasy.

After the Lord dispersed the people by confusing their language, the Bible does not account the raising of a major leader until Abraham. So it is obvious that the only form of serving God they had was what they knew at the time of the Tower of Babel. It is a form of religion in which a man through his own efforts tried to seek after God.

Genesis 11:4:

"And they said, Go to, let us build us a city and a tower, whose top may reach unto heaven; and let us make us a name, lest we be scattered abroad upon the face of the whole earth."

That seemed like a noble idea. The major mistake with this desire of man however is that God did not create us to build a city for ourselves but to help build His city and kingdom. He did not create us to make a name for ourselves but to lift his name up. Whenever we make ourselves or something else the object of our worship instead of God, we raise ourselves in direct confrontation to Him.

Now, many world religions have made man the object of worship. The world encourages self-edification and self-worship as men and women become steeped in selfism and abandon the idea of God as the moral absolute. We are into self-realization, self-development, self-knowledge, self-this, self-that and all we keep hearing is self, self, self.

For those who think it is a mark of modernism to make man the object of worship, it is sobering to realize that this idea of selfism is a very old idea. In the past, when man tried it he reaped confusion just as we are now reaping confusion all over the world. In our efforts to become wise and sophisticated we end up in gross foolishness and blindness! Romans 1:18-32 aptly describes the man who has rejected the true knowledge of God. In verse 28 of that Chapter we read:

> **"And even as they did not like to retain God in their knowledge, God gave them over to reprobate mind, to do those things which are not convenient:"**

When God gives you over to a reprobate mind, you are likely to develop reprobate ideas which would sound reasonable to reprobate people!

Religion

Man's attempt to reach to God resulted in the building of the Tower of Babel. That attempt actually defines the basis of religion which is man's desire and effort to know and relate to God. In every culture of the world there is a "Tower of Babel" which is in the form of beliefs, superstitions, traditions and practices handed down throughout the ages as that society's means of relating to God. Because of that it can be argued that every people have their own way of relating to God.

Acts 17:24-27 helps to explain this concept:

God that made the world and all things therein, seeing that he is Lord of heaven and earth, dwelleth not in temples made with hand;

Neither is worshipped with men's hands, as though he needed any thing, seeing he giveth to all life, and breath, and all things;

And hath made of one blood all nations of men for to dwell on all the face of earth, and hath determined the times before appointed, and the bounds of their habitation;

That they should seek the Lord, if haply they might feel after him, and find him, though he be not far from every one of us:

As strange as that may sound, the Bible teaches that there was a time when God allowed all nations and people to try and seek after Him. So the Indians developed their religious systems as well as the Chinese, the Africans, Europeans, Romans, Greeks and so on. All these religious forms were and are still "Towers of Babel."

At the base of all religions, there are very similar principles and practices because all men originated from one source and have some basic understanding of the requirements of God. For example, almost all world beliefs practice a form of blood sacrifice for atonement, operate a priesthood and believe in covenants.

The major problem that religion presents is that it is man's effort to seek after God and not God's effort to seek after man. Jesus Christ did not seek after man. God is not interested in man's religion. He wants to relate to man by revealing Himself to us and not we trying vainly to seek Him out. Jesus Christ did not begin a religion but revealed God to us, in order to bring to us a new relationship with the Father. In verse 30 of Acts 1 7 the Bible says:

"And the times of this ignorance God winked at; but now commandeth all men every where to repent."

The times of all men everywhere trying to seek after God is described as the times of ignorance! Contrary to popular opinion which tries to label man's Tower of Babel as the "age of enlightenment", God calls it plain ignorance!

Now God is calling people everywhere to turn around and see what He is doing. That is what repentance means. It is an about face! When he made Himself known to Abraham, it was a turn around for all men. He put aside all the confusion from Babel to establish a new order. Abraham did not practice a "religion" but received a revelation and a relationship.

He was called from the Ur of the Chaldees. This was a land much noted for sorcery, magic and idolatry. In those days being a Chaldean was synonymous to being a sorcerer or magician. It was as if that whole nation was totally sold out to worship all kinds of spirits and gods. They were not the only nation practicing this form of religion, but a true representation of the world situation at that time.

Idol worship is not the way to God for any people, be they Incas, Anglo-Saxons, Goths, Aztecs or Africans! It is simply as the Bible describes it, reprobate! As a result of this world-wide apostasy, God chose Abraham to be the Father and Progenitor of a new people and a new revelation which would bring the nations back to God.

Get Thee Out

Now the Lord had said Abram, get thee out of thy country, and from thy kindred, and from thy father's house, unto a land that I will show thee.
Genesis 12:1

The Lord had to break Abram's linkage to his ancestral home and environment in order to receive a fresh revelation of God. The command was strong-Get thee out! His first promise to Abram was:

"And I will make of thee a great nation, and I will bless thee, and make thy name great; and thou shalt be a blessing: And I will bless them that bless thee, and curse him that curseth thee: and in thee shall all families of the earth be blessed."

God took Abram from the Old nation in order to build a New nation through him. The Old nation did not know the true God, but the New nation would receive a true revelation of God. The Old nation was reprobate but the New nation would be approved and accepted of God. The Old nation built its own kingdom, and the New would build God's Kingdom and establish His rule and policies on the face of the earth.

An Altar Unto The Lord

Abram was 75 years old when he heard from God, so in all probability he had lived for 75 years without hearing from God and yet practiced a form of religion. It is interesting to note the progress of understanding he had on his journey towards faith in God. Genesis 12:6-8 explained:

And Abram passed through the land unto the place of Sichem, unto the plain of Moreh. And the Canaanite was then in the land.

> **And the LORD appeared unto Abram, and said, Unto thy seed will I give this land: and there builded he an altar unto the LORD, who appeared unto him,**

> **And he removed from thence unto a mountain on the east of Bethel, and pitched his tent, having Bethel on the west, and Hai on the east: and he builded an altar unto the LORD, and called upon the name of the LORD.**

Note the phrase: "*and there builded he an altar unto the LORD who appeared unto him..*" He first hears from God, then he has a revelation of God and then builds an altar to the Lord and calls upon His name. So now God is not just the voice he heard, or the vision he saw, or the being he worships but Someone he knows on a name basis. It is a growth into an intimate relationship. God is not the "*unknown God*" as the Athenians in Acts chapter 17 understood Him to be, which simply means the unrevealed God, but to Abram He was the revealed God. It is important to note the number of times Abram builds altars to the Lord. He was an intense man of worship.

Melchizedek

After Abram had grown in relationship to God, he came into contact with a strange individual called Melchizedek. I do not intend to do a full teaching on Melchizedek in this book but to highlight his influence on Abram. This is how the Bible introduces him:

Genesis 14:18-20:

And Melchizedek king of Salem brought forth bread and wine: and he was the priest of the most high God.

And he blessed him, and said, Blessed be Abram of the most high God, possessor of heaven and earth:

And blessed be the most high God, which hath delivered thine enemies into thy hand. And he gave him tithes of all."

Actually there are only three verses written directly of him, although later on, the Holy Spirit uses other Biblical writers to cast some more light on him. His Name means King of Righteousness.

The first thing to note is that he was a priest onto the Most High God. Secondly, he was the *King of Salem*, which literally means the *King of Peace*. Thirdly, he knew about the bread and wine which would later symbolize the Seal of the New Covenant. Moreover, he had the ability to impart blessings to Abram and also received tithes from Abram. All these point to the fact that Melchizedek was greater than Abram.

The writer of Hebrews likens his priesthood to the priesthood of Jesus. Hebrews 6:20:

"Whither the forerunner is for us entered, even Jesus, made an high priest forever, after the order of Melchizedek."

In other words the priesthood of Jesus was patterned after the priesthood which was established by Melchizedek. His priestly order pre-dated the Levitical priesthood. It was a priesthood which did not depend on the tribe of Levi, but on the Sovereign call of God on an individual. This is the kind of priesthood that operates under the New Testament. It is generally held that this man was a manifestation of Christ especially when you consider Hebrews 7:1-3:

"For this Melchizedek, King of Salem, priest of the most high God, who met Abraham returning from the slaughter of the kings, and blessed him;

To whom also Abraham gave a tenth part of all first being by interpretation King of righteousness and after that also King of Salem, which is, King of peace;

Without father, without mother, without descent, having neither beginning of days, nor end of life; but made like unto the Son of God abideth a priest continually."

It was through Abraham's relationship with Melchizedek, who I believe was actually Christ, that he received the Laws and ordinances of God to be imparted to the world.

He Will Command His Children

The question I would want to ask is why did God choose Abraham for this purpose? First, God wanted to choose Abraham. This kind of choice is what the Grace of God is all about. Abraham could also be depended on to transfer this knowledge of God to all men. This is what He Himself said about Abraham in Genesis 18:19:

"For I know him, that he will command his children and his household after him, and they shall keep thc way of the LORD to do justice and judgements that the Lord may bring upon Abraham that which he hath spoken of him."

Abraham could be trusted to impart everything he knew to the next generation. Even before he ever had any children of his own, he trained his domestic servants with military skills to be a formidable fighting machine as recorded in Genesis 14:14-16:

And when Abram heard that his brother was taken captive, he armed his trained servants, born in his own house, three hundred and eighteen, and pursued them unto Dan.

And he divided himself against them, he and his servants, by night, and smote them, and pursued them unto Hobah which is on the left hand of Damascus.

And he brought back all the goods, and also brought again his brother Lot, and his goods, and the women also, and the people.

Any man who could train 318 servants, which had been born in his house, to defeat a four-nation allied contingent, can be trusted to train his own children with the truth to take over the nations of the world.

That is an important lesson for Christian parents. Our children should be morally and skillfully trained with the knowledge we have, for the continuity of God's Kingdom. It is depressing to see the looseness and permissiveness some of us tolerate in our homes. Many Christian parents have effectively relinquished their authority to Rock Stars, Television and house-maids! We do not even know what our kids are learning at school, and the sort of pollution our educational system churns out for the gullible consumption of our enthusiastic and neglected children.

The funny thing is, we get shocked when these kids we always thought were "princes" and "princesses" start letting out streams of profanity and obscenity from those pious-looking lips. The truth is, if you do not fill your children with the principles of the Kingdom of God, they will be filled with the principles of the god of this world!

Satan has an agenda for your children - to steal, kill and destroy them right under your roof! He may not physically terminate their lives but he will sow within their hearts and minds seeds of self-destruction which would manifest as they grow up.

It's time to arm our children with truth, sincerity, honesty, boldness and faith in God to move mountains and destroy the armies of satanic philosophies that are taking whole generations captive. Your home should be a boot-camp for God's army!

Enlarging the Promise

After Abram had met Melchizedek, God entered into covenant with him and then through the insistence of his wife, Sarah he had a child with his maid servant, Hagar. God appeared to Abram again and changed his name. Genesis 17:1-8 states:

And when Abram was ninety years old and nine, the LORD appeared to Abram, and said unto him, I am the Almighty God; walk before me, and be thou perfect.

And I will make my covenant between me and thee, and I will multiply thee exceedingly.

And Abram fell on his face: and God talked with him, saying

As for me, behold my covenant is with thee, and thou shalt be a father of many nations.

Neither shall thy name any more be called Abram, but thy name shall be Abraham; for a father of many nations have I made thee.

And I will make thee exceeding fruitful and I will make nations of thee, and kings shall come out of thee.

And I will establish my covenant between me and thee and thy seed after thee in their generations for an everlasting covenant, to be a God unto thee and to thy seed after thee.

And I will give unto thee, and to thy seed after thee, the land wherein thou art a stranger, all

**the land of Canaan, for an everlasting posses-
sion; and I will be their God.**

This promise and blessing was an enlargement on
the first promise. In the first promise God said to
Abram: ***"I will make a great nation out of you."*** It
was simply a blessing that involved one nation.
Through obedience He inherited a greater blessing
"Father of Many Nations." Verse 7 actually is a declaration of God's Covenant Commitment to all of
Abraham's children across the generations. It was not
only to Isaac, but to all the nations that Abraham
would father.

When God speaks of Nations, He may not necessarily be referring to multitudes of people. Most of the
time His references to nations are to individuals who
are not even born yet. By His essential nature, God
sees the end from the beginning and greatness from
little. He sees the conclusion at the beginning and a
forest from a tiny seed.

When we understand this nature of God we are
better able to relate to His promises and prophecies.
Because He abides in an ever-present state, He relates
to yesterday, today and forever not as three different
time periods, but as one eternal *Now*.

When Isaac's wife Rebecca was pregnant the Lord
said unto her:

**"...Two Nations are in thy womb, and two
manner of people shall be separated from thy
bowels..."** Genesis 25:23

What would be your reaction if your wife received such a prophecy? The words first conjure the imagery of a woman pregnant with many tiny ant-sized humans who are divided into two nations. How can an ordinary woman conceive two nations in her womb? The next verse says:

"And when her days to be delivered were fulfilled, behold, there were twins in her womb."

Imagine that! God called twins two nations. To the Lord, one individual baby was a nation and the other was another nation. Can you hear Isaac telling his neighbors,

"Hey, my wife just gave birth to two nations." The neighbors would either totally disbelieve him or run as fast as possible to see the circus spectacle, only to be introduced to a normal healthy set of twins! "Where are the two nations?" They would ask. Isaac would then be the puzzled one and then answer "that's them lying there, can't you see?"

By this time Isaac would have learned God's language and understood how He uses tenses. The neighbors would then walk off murmuring, "That Isaac is real crazy now, calling those twins, nations. I hear his father used to call himself "father of many nations" when he had only one child!" The problem would be that Isaac was talking God's language and neighbors were talking ordinary people's language.

When God changed Abram's name to Abraham, it was an allusion to the fact that all the children that would be fathered by Abraham would be nations, and that those nations would be part of His covenant with Abraham.

When God makes a covenant, so far as the conditions are kept, He will honor it. His Covenant of Redemption was established with Isaac because he was the Son of Promise. The keeping of the Redemption Covenant with Isaac did not nullify God's commitment to the other seed of Abraham. Listen to what God says concerning Ishmael:

And also of the son of the bond-woman will I make a nation, because he is thy seed.
Genesis 21:13

Ishmael became one of the nations that Abraham fathered, because he was a son of the Father of many nations. Although Ishmael was not the covenant child, he still had a stake in the blessing of his father. The Ishmaelites may not necessarily inherit the spiritual blessings of Abraham, but they certainly have the material blessing!

Between Isaac and Ishmael, Abraham fathered two nations which does not really impress me as many. If Abraham was the Father of Many Nations, then there were other nations he fathered.

4

Keturah - The Third Woman

Genesis Chapter 25 begins with this account:

"Then again Abraham took a wife, and her name was Keturah."

Unlike Hagar who was a bondwoman that Abraham took upon the insistence of Sarah, Keturah is the woman Abraham took of his own will. She was the woman of consolation to Abraham after he lost his first and beloved wife Sarah.

It is rather interesting that almost little or nothing is said or known about this woman. I had actually read the book of Genesis through several times and seen the name Keturah but had never been intrigued enough to further study about her until the Spirit of God brought her to my notice as I studied the Scriptures for Biblical information about the dark skinned race.

The thing that really got my attention was the fact that Abraham had the majority of his children with Keturah.

And she bare him Zimran, and Jokshan, and Medan, and Midian, and Ishbak, and Shuah.
Genesis 25:2

Six children in all; which means that six nations were fathered by Abraham through Keturah. I feel like shouting, ('wow!') considering that before the birth of Isaac the body of Abraham was described as dead in Romans 4:19.

I would think that as Abraham saw the developing romance between his son Isaac and his newly married wife Rebecca, he somehow got the notion that his over one hundred and twenty five year old body should not be a hindrance to his dreams. The initial joy and fulfillment Abraham had during his days with Keturah is evidenced in the name of their first child, Zimran, meaning Musical.

The name also prophetically referred to a special grace gifting that would characterize the race that Keturah and Zimran belonged to. Judging from the names of the other children it seems Abraham and Keturah later might have had problems in their marriage. Jokshan means "Insidious;" Medan, "Strife;" Midian, "fighter;" Ishbak, "quit." The name of the last child indicates that finally the apparently young, active and vibrant Keturah submitted to the old and experienced Abraham. The name Shuah implies "to be humble." Shuah is sometimes rendered as Sheba in the Bible.

Since the genealogy of Keturah is not accounted for in the Bible, we would have to trace her lineage through the names of her descendants . In Genesis 25:3 we read:

> **"And Jokshan begat Sheba and Dedan. And the sons of Dedan were Asshurim, and Letushim, and Leummim."**

Jokshan was the second child of Keturah so Sheba and Dedan were grandchildren of Abraham and Keturah. These two grandchildren possessed names that belonged to Cushites or black people. For further light on this explanation we would need to backtrack a bit to Genesis Chapters 9 and 10.

Is the Black Race Cursed?

Before we continue with Keturah, we have to settle a very disturbing controversy "Is the black race cursed?" The first verse we read in Genesis Chapter 9 is:

> **"And God blessed Noah and his sons, and said to them, Be fruitful, and multiply, and replenish the earth."**

It is explicit from the Scriptures that all three sons of Noah were blessed with their father after they survived the flood, to begin a new generation of men. The Bible also makes it abundantly clear that all the human generations of the earth were spawned by these three blessed sons of Noah; Shem, Ham and Japheth.

Later on, the Bible records an incident which over the years has been used by Satan and his agents to teach a doctrine of superiority and inferiority of races and established hideous governmental systems like apartheid.

It is a sad commentary on Christianity, that these theories were supported by some clergy and instituted through the help of some organized Churches. In order to know the truth, we must go to the Book itself for the facts. Genesis 9:18-27 states:

And the sons of Noah, that went forth of the ark, were Shem, and Ham, and Japheth: and Ham is the father of Canaan.

These are the three sons of Noah: and of them was the whole earth overspread.

And Noah began to be an husbandman, and he planted a vineyard:

And he drank of the wine, and was drunken; and he was uncovered within his tent.

And Ham, the father of Canaan, saw the nakedness of his father, and told his two brethren without.

And Shem and Japheth took a garment, and laid it upon both their shoulders, and went backward, and covered the nakedness of their father; and their faces were backward, and they saw not their father's nakedness.

And Noah awoke from his wine, and knew what his younger son had done unto him.

> **And he said, Cursed be Canaan; a servant of servants shall he be unto his brethren.**
>
> **And he said, Blessed be the LORD God of Shem; and Canaan shall be his servant.**
>
> **God shall enlarge Japheth, and he shall dwell in the tents of Shem; and Canaan shall be his servant.**

I have taken the liberty to quote this much of Scripture for the avoidance of any doubt. The story is simple. Noah cultivates grapes and later produces wine out of them. He gets drunk on the wine and falls asleep naked in his tent. His second son, Ham, comes along and sees his father's nakedness but instead of covering his father's shame, he goes out to gossip about it to his two other brothers who wisely covered up their father without looking at his nakedness. Noah later wakes up from his sleep finds out what has happened and pronounces corresponding blessings and curses on his family.

My purpose here is not to show the morality of an action but to allow the facts to speak for themselves.

First, let us establish the name of the individual who committed the offence. Verse 22 is clear about that.

> **"And Ham, the father of Canaan, saw the nakedness of his father,...."**

The offense was committed by Ham. Shem and Japheth were those who covered Noah.

The second thing is to find out who was cursed - and with that vs 25 clearly states:

"And he said Cursed be Canaan; a servant of servants shall he be unto his brethren."

Canaan according to Genesis 10:6 was the fourth son of Ham.

Amazing as it may seem, the Bible states that although Ham was the culprit he was never cursed but somehow his fourth son Canaan, who was not the accused, was cursed.

The question then is, why was not Ham cursed? The answer is straight and simple. Ham had already been blessed by Almighty God in Genesis Chapter 9 verse 1, and Noah knew he could not undo that blessing with his curse so he made Canaan the scapegoat for his father's sins.

In Numbers 23:20 Balaam found out that when God blesses, no one can reverse it. If Ham had been cursed, then all his children would have been cursed, but thank God that was not the case. In all, Ham had four children as recorded in Genesis 10:6:

"And the sons of Ham; Cush, and Mizraim, and Phut, and Canaan."

It must be noted that Cush, the first born of Ham was never cursed. Mizraim the second son was never cursed. Phut the third son was never cursed. Only Canaan the fourth son was cursed by Noah. If nothing else, we can say that Cush, as the first born of Ham received a double portion of his father's blessing according to biblical precedence.

It is further enlightening to note that the name Cush also means Ethiopia. He was the father of the black races of the world; and he was never cursed. Full Stop!

Sheba and Dedan

With that explanation on Noah's curse, let us shift our attention back to Keturah's grandchildren, Sheba and Dedan;

And the sons of Cush; Seba and Havilah, and Sabtah, and Raamah, and Sabtecha; and the sons of Raamah; *Sheba and Dedan***"**
Genesis 10:7

Here in this verse Sheba and Dedan are described as being from the Cushite line.

If that is the case, then we can safely deduce that the Sheba and Dedan we read of in the descendants of Keturah were also Cushites. That is strange because Abraham was from the lineage of Shem, so what are these Cushites doing in a Shemite family?

The only conclusion to draw is that Abraham married into a Cushite family through his wife Keturah. That must not sound strange to us, because after the flood, the leaders of the world were Cushites.

This is not to teach the racial superiority of the Cushites but to help us understand that over the years God has chosen to use whom He pleases for His Glory, in spite of the color of their skin. One of the descendants of Cush, by the name of Nimrod was described as a mighty one in the Earth;

And Cush begat Nimrod: he began to be a mighty one in the earth. Genesis 10:8

I wish to submit to you that when the Bible says mighty it means *Mighty*. This Nimrod was the one who united the nations of the world and led them to build the first modern cities after the flood, as found in Genesis 10:9-12.

He was a mighty hunter before the Lord: wherefore it is said, Even as Nimrod the mighty hunter before the LORD.

And the beginning of his kingdom was Babel, and Erech, and Accad, and Calneh, in the land of Shinar.

Out of that land went forth Asshur, and builded Nineveh, and the city of Rehoboth, and Calah,

And Resen between Nineveh and Calah: the same is a great city.

When he said "go to," the nations of the world obeyed. It was his idea to build the tower of Babel which later led to dispersal of the nations. He built kingdoms and established civilizations out of which other cities were built.

There obviously were some things wrong about his system of government and religion which displeased the Lord, but the fact still remains that he was the first governmental leader and motivator mentioned after the flood.

Havilah

Havilah, the second son of Cush, is another name that calls for a closer examination. As we study the book of Genesis, we come across his name associated with a land near to the Garden of Eden.

And a river went out of Eden to water the garden; and from thence it was parted, and became into four heads,

The name of the first is Pison: that is it which compasseth the whole land of Havilah where there is gold. Genesis 2:10-11

The land of Havilah was a Cushite land located close to where the original Garden of Eden was, and it was also a land abounding in much gold. Surprisingly, the second river head mentioned in the Garden of Eden is also connected to a land belonging to Cushites.

"And the name of the second river is Gihon; the same is it that compasseth the whole land of Ethiopia."

Ethiopia and Cush are synonymous, so of the four riverheads that watered the Garden of Eden two are distinctly identified with Cushite lands.

That leads me to ask a very disturbing question? *"Did Almighty God locate the Garden of Eden in a land later to be occupied by black-skinned people?"*

I am not one to fuss about the color of a man's skin because to me, the value of an individual is not in his outer covering, but in the God-inspired spirit that is within him. However, some of these questions come up because of the lie that has been told black people over the years, that they are accursed, second class citizens of the world.

For example, if we agree with the Biblical record, that the body of man was made out of the dust of the earth, it becomes tempting to ask the begging question; What was the color of the clay from which Adam was made? Well as far as I know, it is very difficult to get light pink clay anywhere in the world. It is however, general knowledge that dark brown is more in abundance. You see, if we start emphasizing the outer man instead of the inner man, there would be no end to the confusion. That is why no system should determine human value by the color of the skin.

Let the words of the Apostle Peter after he saw God pour out the Holy Spirit upon Gentiles continually guide us. He said; "Of a truth I perceive that God is no respecter of persons; but in every nation he that feareth him, and worketh righteousness, is accepted with him" Acts 10:34-35.

The Inheritance Of Abraham

As we continue pursuing God's dealings with Abraham and his children, we approach a very symbolic but vital incident that occurs just before the death of Abraham. It involved the distribution of his inheritance to his children.

It is worthy to note that the Abrahamic inheritance was both spiritual and material and was supposed to be passed on from generation to generation. The spiritual aspects of the blessing involved the coming of the Messiah and his redemptive work. The material aspect of the inheritance provided security and prosperity to the people who received it.

Of the eight recorded children of Abraham, only Isaac was directly chosen by God on the basis of His promise and grace to continue the lineage that would later receive the Messiah Jesus Christ.

Genesis 25:5-6 records:

"And Abraham gave all that he had unto Isaac.

But unto the sons of the concubines, which Abraham had, Abraham gave gifts, and sent them away from Isaac his son, while he yet lived, eastward, unto the east country."

As had been promised by God, Isaac received both Spiritual and Material blessing of the Abrahamic inheritance.

Ishmael was given a token gift and sent off but he did not have much to worry about, because earlier on the Lord had occasion to pronounce this blessing on him when Abraham pleaded on his behalf,

And as for Ishmael, I have heard thee: Behold, I have blessed him, and will make him fruitful, and will multiply him exceedingly; twelve princes shall he beget, and I will make him a great nation.   Genesis 17:20

So, although Ishmael did not directly receive a blessing from Abraham, the Lord had seen to it that he would not be lacking material blessings since he was a child of Abraham.

The real losers were Keturah's Cushite children. They did not have material blessing nor were they given the spiritual blessing. They had been taught about the faith of Abraham all right, but they left the presence of their father with only token gifts into the east country. These were the disinherited children of Abraham.

The troubling thing to me was that they were Cushites and my kinsmen after the flesh. They were the majority but the least privileged of Abraham's children. It is most saddening to see these children, Zimran, Jokshan, Medan, Median, Ishbak and Shuah moving most probably with their mother Keturah to the east country.

As a matter of fact when Abraham died they did not attend the funeral. Genesis 25:9 notes Isaac and Ishmael as the ones who were present to bury their father.

As we move along we would discover how God later on restored these Cushite children of Abraham back to the inheritance.

5

Jethro - Keeping The Faith

One of the most baffling and somewhat enigmatic personalities of the Old Testament is Jethro. He appears on the scene in the Book of Exodus as the man who provided refuge for Moses after he was banished from Egypt. His role and influence over the life of Moses is very foundational since it spanned the next forty years, which was featured as the second phase of Moses' life and ministry. To me those were the most crucial years in the life of the future liberator of the Children of Israel.

The life of Moses can be divided into three periods each made up of forty years. The first forty years were spent in the palace of Pharaoh. The second forty years were spent under the tutelage of Jethro during the wilderness experience. The last forty years were spent leading Israel into the promised land.

Before Moses came into contact with Jethro, he had already spent the first forty years of his life being raised as a royal prince in Egypt. According to Acts 7:22 he was **"...learned in all the wisdom of the Egyptians, and was mighty in words and in deeds."**

As a specially trained Egyptian, his religion had been that of the Egyptians. His faith was in the gods of Egypt. His culture and lifestyle were typically Egyptian. I would further say that as a trained Egyptian, Moses had no personal encounter with the God of Abraham, because even the Hebrews had so much forgotten about their God that they could not remember His Name!

For four hundred years they had grown in a foreign land and imbibed foreign beliefs such as the worship of the Golden Calf, which kept haunting them on their journey to the promised land. Much of the knowledge Abraham, Isaac and Jacob passed on to them concerning the covenant keeping God, had been either forgotten or totally mixed up with the Egyptian religious belief in many gods which actually were demons. The Lord had to later on wipe out the whole generation that came out of Egypt, because they could not get the worship of idols out of their minds and hearts.

In order for God to reveal Himself to Moses, He had to take him out of Egypt and bring him to a new environment, where he could unlearn forty years experience and be properly introduced to the covenant God of Abraham, Isaac, and Jacob. Of all the people and lands in the world God chose the man Jethro of the Land of Midian, to be the mentor to the future Liberator and Law-giver of Israel.

It is an irony of history to realize that of all the children of Abraham it was the disinherited sons of

Keturah who kept the faith of their father. They kept the flames of the Abrahamic flame alive to rekindle hope for Israel. A true case of the stone which the builders rejected becoming the head of the corner.

The Priest

At first encounter in Exodus 2:16 and 3:1; Jethro is described as a Priest. Exodus 18:12 further impresses on us the fact that he was a Priest unto God. So the question is, how come there was a priest of God in Midian? What was a Priest of God doing in Midian when all the covenant people of Israel are locked up in bondage in Egypt? The answer is in the statement of trust God made to Abraham in Genesis 18:19:

"For I know him *Abraham*, that he will command his children and his household after him, and they shall keep the way of the Lord, to do justice and judgment; that the Lord may bring upon Abraham that which He hath spoken of him."

Abraham obtained a report from God as one who had the ability to transfer knowledge from one generation to another. This quality was to serve as a major condition for God fulfilling His promise to Abraham. From our previous study, we established the fact that Midian was a direct son of Abraham through his Cushite wife, Keturah and that makes it easy to understand why at a time when all the knowledge of the true God had been destroyed, Jethro still kept the faith. He was a descendant of Abraham who had obeyed the commands of Abraham concerning the Almighty God! Jethro kept the flame of Abraham's faith burning for Moses to partake of.

The priesthood of Jethro is rather strange. He obtained the priesthood by faith and not by works. The presence of the priesthood implied the presence of a covenant, because the priests were there to mediate the covenant.

It is likely that Abraham was ushered into the priestly ministry after he met Melchizedek, who is the first person expressly described as a priest in the Bible. This ministry of the priest is what Jethro inherited. It is the kind of priesthood we operate in under the New Testament. It is of Faith and Grace, and not of Works. He operated as a priest unto the Lord before Aaron was consecrated priest unto God, and as such before the Levitical priesthood was established. As a matter of fact, he led in the sacrifices in Exodus 18:12:

"And Jethro, Moses' father-in-law, took a burnt offering, and sacrifices for God: and Aaron came, and all the elders of Israel, to eat bread with Moses' father-in-law before God."

It is clear enough here that although Aaron was around when it was time to function in the priestly office, Jethro took the precedence.

Teacher

The priests' ministry according to Malachi 2:7 involved the teaching of the Law of God - **"For the priest's lips should keep knowledge, and they should seek the law at his mouth: for he is the messenger of the LORD of hosts."**

There is a statement that Moses made in Exodus 18:16 which helps to enlighten us concerning a possible aspect of Jethro's ministry which has been overlooked. In response to Jethro's enquiry as to why he had to personally attend to all the problems of Israel, Moses said, in Exodus 18:16:

"When they have a matter, they come unto me; and I judge between one and another, *and I do make them know the statutes of God, and His laws,"*

This is strange because Moses is making this statement before the giving of the Law on Mount Sinai; implying that before God engraved the Law on tablets to Israel, He made part of the Law known to Moses. The obvious question is, how did Moses get to know of the Law of God before Mount Sinai? Who taught him?

In order to answer that question we need to realize the difference between the Abrahamic Covenant and the Mosaic Covenant. Under the Abrahamic Covenant, faith based on an intimate relationship with God was the operative principle. Under the Mosaic

Law, obedience through a strict adherence to a written code was the operative principle.

Under the Abrahamic Covenant, it was not necessary for the individual to have a written code in order to obey God. Relationship with the Lord guaranteed obedience to God. Actually, what God encoded at Mount Sinai was known by Abraham. For example he tithed and taught his children to tithe before tithing was instituted as a law in Israel through the Mosaic Law. Jethro operated under the Abrahamic Covenant and so, had a knowledge of the Law of God because of that intimate relationship he enjoyed.

It is obvious that as his part in continuing the Abrahamic heritage, he also commanded his household, of which Moses was a part, to walk in the statutes and ways of Almighty God. *He was a law-giver to Moses.*

I can almost see him painstakingly recounting God's dealings with Abraham to Moses; about how God took him out of a nation of idol worshippers and sorcerers to found a new nation who would serve and worship the One True God. These would appear as strange concepts to Moses who, although had a sense of destiny in his life was really mixed up in his theology.

Precept upon precept, line upon line, here a little, there a little, Jethro helped his protege discard false beliefs and false confidence in the Egyptian gods of the flies, snake, Nile and other deities. His confidence as a man-made royal prince was broken to the extent that contrary to his description as a man who was trained to be mighty in words, when he finally had a personal encounter with God, he said;

> **O my Lord, I am not eloquent, neither heretofore, nor since thou hast spoken unto thy servant: but I am slow of speech, and of a slow tongue.** Exodus 4:10

This was a new Moses who was ready to be nothing, so that God would be everything to him. I believe the ministry of present day Jethros are still needed to teach the nations and leaders of nations the Ways of the Lord.

Wise Counselor

I would guess that one of the most memorable acts of Jethro was the counsel he gave to Moses on how to organize the multitudes he had delivered from slavery. In that counsel, he established a very vital management principle which has been assimilated into the administration of schools, companies and nations.

In the church world, it is severally referred to as *'home fellowship,' 'cell groups' or 'care groups."* It is a system of administration that builds up from the bottom to the top.

If the description of Israel in Acts 7:38 as the Church in the wilderness is anything to go by, then Jethro can be referred to as the first one to introduce Church government to Israel.

I have always wondered why Moses did not know about that System of Administration since he was involved in government in Egypt and had been trained as a Statesman. It is important to note that at this point in time Egypt was the center of civilization, yet Moses in his forty years as a Statesman in Egypt did not have a working knowledge of this principle. This simply confirms that Jethro did not receive that knowledge from the institutions of his day but as a direct Wisdom from Almighty God.

When you understand that Jethro was of the Cushite or black race, then it makes nonsense of the assumption that black people cannot govern themselves. The nation of Israel, and for that matter all nations owe this black priest an honor for being the vessel through whom principles of local government administration were established.

Moses' Father-In-Law

I would think that Moses was most honored by the fact that this humble Priest of God was his father-in-law. In Exodus 2:21 we read the account of Moses' marriage:

"And Moses was content to dwell with the man *Jethro* : and he gave Moses Zipporah his daughter."

Well I do not blame Jethro. If I knew who was going to be God's man with such a powerful ministry, I think

I would also let him marry my daughter! That is wisdom!!

In a sense, the fact of Moses being married to Jethro's daughter gives one of the clearest biblical indications as to the natural race of Jethro. As we read in Numbers 12:1:

"And Miriam and Aaron spake against Moses because of the Ethiopian woman whom he had married: for he had married an Ethiopian woman."

This is plain black and white in the Bible. Moses married a black woman; definitely if Moses' wife was an Ethiopian then Moses' father-in-law was an Ethiopian or *black*.

Unfortunately, many people, even theologians who have all along propagated the idea of the superiority of the Caucasian race and the inferiority of the Negroid race, find this Biblical account too bitter a pill to swallow that they have tried to project an argument to the effect that this woman was not Zipporah but a second wife. This interpretation is totally dishonest. It would have been a normal Biblical practice to have recorded the name of the woman if she was a new wife.

A little background information to the story will help us understand why Miriam and Aaron had to protest at this point in time and not previously.

It is obvious that when Moses left Egypt at the age of forty he was not married. The Bible does not give us any indication of any earlier marriage contracted by Moses prior to his marriage to Zipporah. It is also helpful to note that although Moses was raised as an Egyptian in Pharaoh's palace, his immediate natural family knew him as their kin because the Bible accounts that his sister Miriam saw the Pharaoh's daughter picking him up from the river.

Later on, his real mother was hired as nurse to nurture him. Exodus 2:1-10. During the next forty years when he was domiciled in the Land of Midian, they apparently lost touch with him until he encountered Aaron by a divine appointment after receiving his commission to liberate Israel.

In Exodus 18:2, 5 we read this account:

> **Then Jethro, Moses' father-in-law, took Zipporah, Moses wife, *after he had sent her back*,**
>
> **And her two sons;...**
>
> **And Jethro, Moses' father-in-law, came with his sons and his wife unto Moses into the wilderness, where he encamped at the Mount of God."**

From these verses we gather that Moses had to send his wife and kids back to his father-in-law somewhere during his return journey to Egypt and pursued his God-given Mission alone.

It is most probable that Zipporah returned home after the incidents recorded in Exodus 4:20-26. It was then necessary for Jethro to bring the family of Moses back to him after the deliverance of Israel.

That was the first time that any of the people of Israel actually set eyes on the family of Moses and the color of their skin.

It is almost certain that Miriam and Aaron who had by then assumed the role as the closest family and confidants of Moses were peeved to see the honor Moses gave to his Mentor, Jethro, and the influence of his counsel to Moses. They also would be most disturbed when Moses pleaded with his wife's family to be the 'eyes' or scouts to Israel on their wilderness journey. Numbers 10:29-32.

As in the case with people when their positions of power seem threatened, Miriam and Aaron then started finding faults with the skin color of Zipporah, and by inference her family. That critical statement gives us the clearest indication of the race of Jethro, Zipporah and the rest of Jethro's children, such as Hobab.

Hobab - The Scouter

The reason we are going at lengths to establish the racial identity of Jethro's family is to bring us into an understanding of God's faithfulness to His promise to Abraham's children. Although the children of Keturah had been disinherited by Abraham, God had to re-establish the broken links in His process of restoring their lost inheritance.

Proverbs 17:2 teaches a biblical principle for obtaining an inheritance:

"A wise servant shall have rule over a son that causeth shame, and shall have part of the inheritance among the brethren."

Through wisdom and service, an individual could obtain an inheritance from his brethren. This is the principle God used in the case of the disinherited children of Abraham, in order to restore them to their inheritance among brethren.

Jethro provided wisdom through his counsel to Moses and his son Hobab provided the service. It is very logical to reason that on his visit to Moses in the wilderness, Jethro brought along with him other members of the family, for we find in Numbers 10:29-32 this account:

And Moses said unto Hobab, the son of Raguel [Raguel is the other name of Jethro] the Midianite, Moses' father in law, We are journeying unto the place of which the LORD said, I will give it you: come thou with us, and we will do thee good: for the LORD hath spoken good concerning Israel.

And he said unto him, I will not go; but I will depart to mine own land, and to my kindred.

And he said, Leave us not, I pray thee; forasmuch as thou knowest how we are to encamp in the wilderness, and thou mayest be to us instead of eyes.

And it shall be, if thou go with us, yea, it shall be, that what goodness the LORD shall do unto us, the same will we do unto thee.

Moses literally offered his Midianite brother-in-law the opportunity to regain their portion in the Abrahamic inheritance. This was because after the counsel of Jethro, Moses still realized that the Midianites were needed to use their skill and knowledge of the desert terrain to guide and protect Israel on their pilgrimage. The Midianites, as their name implied were also very good fighters.

If Hobab and his brethren accepted the challenge then Moses promised:

"What goodness the Lord shall do unto us, the same will we do unto thee."

At this point in time, Hobab was the Key to obtaining the inheritance. If he took up the challenge to serve Israel as Scout and guide along the tortuous wilderness, and literally be the *eye* that provides vision for that nation, then these representatives of Abraham's Cushite children will get back to the inheritance!

Did he Go? Did he provide that service to Israel? Let us find out!

6

Rediscovering Our Inheritance

Throughout Israel's wanderings in the wilderness not much is heard about Hobab and his people; until they got into the promised land. There, when the inheritance of the tribes were being allotted, we read this account.

Judges 1:16 states:

"And the children of the Kenite, Moses' father-in-law, went up out of the city of palm trees with the children of Judah into the wilderness of Judah, which lieth in the south of Arad; and they went and dwelt among the people."

In this passage the Midianites are referred to by their other synonymous name - Kenite. Black people in the Promised Land? Yes! The land flowing with milk and honey? Yes! Sharing the inheritance with Judah? Yes!

The children of Midian featured prominently in God's dealings with Israel.

When it was time for God to fulfill His purpose of bringing Israel into Egypt, He used a Midianite group to take Joseph into Egypt. It was through Joseph that the rest of Israel got into Egypt.

A Midianite priest was used to prepare Moses to deliver Israel from bondage.

God again used the same Midianites to get them to the promised land. Is it coincidence? No, this is called *Divine Purpose!*

If they got to the promised land, then it means that Hobab took up the challenge of Moses to become an *eye* to Israel. He and his people not only gave organizational structure to Israel; they also provided vision.

For forty years they offered supportive ministry to Moses. Moses had the word about the promised land but did not know how to get there. God never gives to one man everything. That is why we have to open up to receive from others, the deposit that God has made into their lives.

I know somebody is going to ask the obvious question, "What about the Bible saying that Israel was led by the Cloud of Glory and the presence of God?" Well, do you not think if anyone knew that fact it would be Moses? Yet he asked Hobab to be an eye to Israel. Just because you are led by the Spirit of God does not mean you would never need a man's help.

The Cloud of Glory gave Israel indications as to when to move or stop. Hobab was used by God to help them know specific places to encamp and prepare the way before them.

Joshua kept the covenant Moses made with Hobab. It was in fulfillment of God's Covenant with Abraham and the nations that he would father. Midian, a black son of Abraham and Keturah, is now in the inheritance where he belongs.

The full significance of this restoration is found in the words of Moses.

In Exodus Chapter 3 verse 12, God made a covenant with Moses to teach his mouth what to say. It is with this same mouth that he covenanted with Hobab.

And it shall be, if thou go with us, yea, it shall be, that what goodness the Lord shall do unto us, the same will we do unto thee.
Numbers 10:32

It was a covenant of equal sharing; the same level of blessing. So let us find out the inheritance of Judah so as to know the inheritance of the Cushite children of Abraham.

Praise

In the first place this is how Judah got his name.

And she conceived again, and bare a son: and she said, Now will I praise the LORD: therefore

she called his name Judah and left bearing.
Genesis 29:35

The name of Judah meant Praise. Furthermore there was this prophecy in Genesis 49:8:

"Judah, thou art he whom thy brethren shall praise: thy hand shall be in the neck of thine enemies; thy father's children shall bow down before thee."

In other words, not only would Judah be a man of praise, but he would also be praised because of his exalted position among his brethren.

The leadership of Old Testament praise and worship was mostly taken by Judah. The Great Psalmist David, whose prophetic songs have been of blessing to us throughout the ages, was from the Tribe of Judah.

The Ministry of Praise, by its nature involves a lot of music and drama. It is artistic.

Can you understand why black people are so full of music, rhythm and dance? Whereas other people take many dance lessons to be able to move their limbs in rhythm to music, a black person will simply flow! The music is in them. It is an inheritance.

Wherever they find themselves - in the Caribbean, Europe, America, Africa and other places - music rolls out of them. This must explain why Abraham's first son with Keturah was called Zimran, which means musical. As the first born son, Zimran carried that ability on behalf of all his brothers.

We are so full of music that when our ancestors were taken into slavery and pressed on every side, out of them oozed what was in them; music! This form of music that was later called Negro Spirituals. They did not produce carnality, they produced spirituals out of the abundance of what was in them. Go to any authentic black congregation - some of them may not preach right, but they sure will sing the anointing upon you!

It is through praise and worship that the presence of God is released amongst His people. Unfortunately when the missionaries came in, they put aside our music and brought in their sedate and unexciting music forms, but thank God the music is coming back to the church. The church world has not experienced real praise and worship yet, because the people to lead it have spent much of their time imitating substitutes.

Our churches should write fresh hymns and spiritual songs with our flavour, and let the nations of the world be blessed through this great heritage. Brothers, let the music flow; sisters, let the music flow. Let's bring our offering of praise to the Altar and throne of the King of Kings and the Great Liberator.

The prophecy of the prophet Zephaniah, who is himself presented in Zephaniah 1:1 as the son of Cushi, must be literally fulfilled when he declared by the Spirit;

From beyond the rivers of Ethiopia My suppliants, even the daughter of my dispersed, shall bring mine offering.   Zephaniah 3:10

Messianic Line

Genesis 49:9-11 reads:

Judah is a lion's whelp: from the prey, my son, thou art gone up: he stooped down, he couched as a lion, and as an old lion; who shall rouse him up?

The Sceptre shall not depart from Judah, nor a law giver from between his feet, until Shiloh come; and unto him shall the gathering of the people be.

Binding his foal unto the vine, and his ass's colt unto the choice vine; he washed his garment in wine, and his clothes in the blood of grapes.

This prophecy introduces Judah as a Lion, which denotes boldness. The prophecy also establishes Judah as the bearer of the Sceptre and the Lawgiver which is reference to Kingship. Most importantly it identifies Judah as the tribe from which *"Shiloh"* - the presence of God or Immanuel-shall come. Did the inheritance of Keturah's children include all these? Oh yes it did! It literally linked up these black people with God's purposes in bringing redemption to humanity.

It is as if God was saying, *"Abraham did not give you an inheritance, he sent you off but I am going to put you in the center of my redemption plan to bring salvation to mankind."* This blessing was not a physical blessing. It was a spiritual blessing. It did not necessarily make them naturally prosperous, but the truth is that the natural is always produced from the spiritual. It is the anointing that breaks the yoke! I believe the total liberation of black people will be preceded by a major revival of God's power and glory in the nations.

When Jesus was born, wise men from the East came to pay homage. It is believed that these people were black people who were part of Keturah's children that were sent off to the east country by Abraham. Gen. 25:6.

As a result of black people's connection to God's plan of redemption, it was necessary for a black man to help Christ carry the cross to Cavalry.

And as they came out, they found a man of Cyrene, Simon by name: him they compelled to bear his cross. Matthew 27:32 *(mark 15: 2)*

It was necessary for Simon to be where he was and be found, just as it was necessary for the Midianite caravan to be around and be found to take Joseph into Egypt. That is no co-incidence. As you may be aware, Jesus was naturally from Judah, which had a link with Midian.

On the day of Pentecost, there were black people around who heard the Gospel preached in their own language.

Even before Cornelius could receive the Gospel as the first Gentile, God had to keep covenant with black people by letting them hear it first. Cornelius was a Roman and therefore an European. Before he knew about God's redemption offer through the Lord Jesus Christ, the Ethiopian Eunuch had experienced Salvation.

God had to take Philip from a whole city-wide crusade to get one lone Ethiopian! Africa got the Gospel before Europe. He is a Covenant keeping God!

The influence of black people on Christianity's great Apostle is recorded in Acts 13:1-3:

> **Now there were in the church that was at Antioch certain prophets and teachers; as Barnabas, and Simeon that was called Niger, and Lucius of Cyrene, and Manaen, which had been brought up with Herod the tetrarch, and Saul.**

> **As they ministered to the Lord, and fasted, the Holy Ghost said, Separate me Barnabas and Saul for the work whereunto I have called them.**

> **And when they had fasted and prayed, and laid their hands on them, they sent them away.**

Of the five prophets and teachers at this Apostolic Commissioning Service, two are positively identified as black. Simeon called Niger and Lucius of Cyrene, both names of African lands. Of these people who were present, the Holy Spirit said *"Set out Paul and Barnabas."* If logic will serve us any benefit, the likelihood is that the prophecy came from the other three. Of these three, two are positively black people. So who did the Holy Spirit use to give the prophecy? Your guess is as good as mine.

After the prophecy, these other three laid hands on Paul and Barnabas to send them into the mission field. I know some of us cannot imagine those powerful and anointed black hands on the head of Paul. The truth is; it happened! After every missionary journey, Paul would go back to Antioch to give a report to those who sent him.

Well, most of us have grown up thinking all missionary boards are made up of Europeans or people of non-black extraction. The good news is that it is all right for black people to send missionaries into the field. And folks, let's do it!

In these days the Spirit of God is bringing a renewed emphasis into the church. It began with the restoration of the gifts of the Spirit in the early 1900's. This revival is what has birthed Pentecostalism and Charismaticism which is now changing the complexion of Christianity.

That revival was led by William Seymour - a black man! There is a divine purpose for us that Satan has tried to stifle, but this is a new day!

Normally, you will not try to destroy someone who

is poor. No one goes out of his way to destroy a poor or a weak person. You always want to attack the strong. You have to ask yourself; why is it that although the black people are supposed to be weak, everyone attacks them? They are supposed to be weak, poor, not to have anything but it seems that everything is being done to suppress them.

Both on the home continent and out of the home continent, there is a demonic, devilish attack from hell to stop these people from executing their spiritual office. When these people start to stand in that place, there is going to come a light and redemption to the nations.

After preaching some of the information contained in this book the Holy Spirit inspired this prophecy. The occasion was Dr. Myles Munroe's Believers Summit in Nassau, Bahamas.

Saith the Spirit of God, "I will roar Upon the nations again and I will awaken with a shout upon the nations again and I will cause my breath to consume the nations again. For when I find a people who are ready, then my Spirit shall quicken them and I will roar into them with the roar of the lion of boldness and of confidence. For saith the Spirit of God you have been timid for too long and you have sat in a corner for too long but it is time to rise with a roar and with a shout."

For saith the Lord, "your voice has not been heard in the nations, your voice has not been heard in the continents. The rivers of life in you have not been drank by the nations so shake yourself out of that misery and shake yourself out of that pity and shake yourself out of that social bondage, for I will cause the Lion of Judah to rise with you and you shall roar like a young lion, and like a young lion you shall move forth and you shall do great things for me as you turn your face and as you turn round" saith the Lord.

"He that has an eye let him see what the Spirit is doing, for I am causing a new wind and that new wind is blowing from a place you never see a wind blow from, that new wind is blowing from a place that was despised. For I will cause my sons and daughters with my anointing and with my power, to move forth in the nations of the world and the world shall be blessed because of them, for the time has come for the nations to be helped.

For who shall bind the wind of the Spirit of God and who shall restrain the wind of the Spirit of God and who shall programme the Spirit of God, for the wind bloweth where it listeth so does my Spirit. For who shall command me concerning my doings, who shall command me concerning whom I use. For who shall command me whom I send, for I will use whom I will use and I will send whom I send and I will bless whom I will bless saith the Lord, and I will cause my face to shine upon whom I want to shine upon for I have chosen a people looked down upon, despised and a people spat upon and I have put my glory upon them and have anointed them and through the anointing shall they inherit their inheritance" saith God.

"*If you will be diligent and walk in that anointing and not in the arm of flesh, and walk in that Spirit and not in programmes, and if you will be diligent to seek my face and to walk in the power of my Spirit, so shall your inheritance burst forth upon you for I am doing a new thing. I am doing a new thing, I am doing something which has not been done before. I am rising upon a people who have not been risen upon before, and I will complete my work and I will cause my people to be in the place that I want them to be, sit in the place I want them to sit saith the Lord. The hour is come for those who were hidden to be manifested.*""

Hallelujah! Glory to God! It's a new day!

7

Blessed To Bless

The purpose of God for blessing any individual is to use that person as a conduit of His blessing. God does not bless you for yourself - He blesses you for others. We receive His blessing and visitation so we can contribute our portion to humanity. You do not go about shouting "Bless God, I'm blessed," and just feel good about it; being blessed carries the responsibility of channeling that blessing to others.

God said to Abram in Genesis 12:2:

> **"And I will make of thee a great nation, and I will bless thee, and make thy name great and thou shalt be a blessing."**

Note those words: *"and thou shalt be a blessing."*

How can an individual be a blessing when he is always receiving and never giving?

How can you give except you have something to give? How can you give to the person who gave you all you have?

If what you have is what someone gave to you then you cannot give it back to him, because he already had it before he gave it to you.

It is difficult to be a blessing to a person you are always receiving from. In that situation, you become the receiver of the blessing instead of the giver of the blessing.

If you want to give anything that has worth, it must be original, unique and "home-brewed"; and you cannot be unique while you spend all your life following, copying and imitating.

When the Lord called me to pioneer a church, He impressed on me strongly to found a church that would not be tied to the apron-strings of a foreign financing mission board.

The Lord called me to teach my congregation to stop looking to Europe or America as the source of supply, but to cultivate a new spirit and ethic of national development. I fully believe that wherever God puts you, He has enough resources in place to take care of your needs. As a result of that conviction, our church has pursued a vigorous policy of indigenous financing and government.

I do not believe the church in Africa should be ruled from anywhere but Africa! Our leaders must be *"home brewed."* Our finances must be generated from the productive work of our own resources. Our headquarters must be Africa! When it becomes necessary to co-operate with other churches and ministries beyond our continent, it must be based on mutual respect and love. We were not made in God's image to receive "mercy drops!"

The times have changed and God is calling on us to change our attitudes and expectations.

Independence

The late 1950's and early 1960's were landmark years for many dark-skinned people. Many nations in black Africa became independent from their colonial masters, and in the United States the Civil Rights movement got some legislation passed to integrate black people into the mainstream of the society.

The simple idea that we became independent implies that before then, we were dependent. This brings up very serious facts for consideration, because dependency is a crippling condition that makes one individual or group look up to another for help and support.

Dependency also develops through the process of addiction to a substance, an idea or a person. Any person who is hooked, for example, to hard drugs, uses dependency on that substance as the means for survival. This survivalist attitude will make that individual steal, lie, kill and destroy anyone including himself in order to get the substance he depends on. Although he could be aware of the destructive nature of his dependence, the price of freedom would mean going through a tortuous withdrawal process which may appear worse than the dependency.

For such a person no declaration, vow or promise will free him. What am I then saying? It is simply this; it takes a long process to make you dependent and it will take a longer fighting process to make you independent. Dependency cannot be broken overnight, neither can it be overruled by just a mere paper or legislation. In other words, declaring independence does not in any way mean freedom from dependency. I think this is something most Third World nations are beginning to understand. The process that made us dependent has so much addicted us to certain concepts and conditions that now we find ourselves in a situation I describe as "bondage in freedom." The most difficult part to break in any situation of addiction and dependency is not the physical but the mental, so then mental slavery is more difficult to break than physical slavery.

The minds of our people are so hooked on the supply and superiority of the white skin that it is almost impossible for them to conceive the thought of standing on their own two feet. Whenever they attempt to stand, they would still want to hold the hands of the "old-master." With that attitude, no economic policy will take root and function.

A dependent man cannot be trusted. He would shout loud slogans but never settle to produce. Unfortunately, the church harbors a large number of dependent pastors and members who are not ready to go through the pain of breaking new frontiers and establishing new foundations. That was the problem God had with Israel. At the least opposition or hardship, they thought of their former slave-master Egypt. God had to wipe out a whole generation in order to raise a new generation who had a different spirit to conquer.

Although the Spirit of God is signifying that this is our time, there is little that our generation can achieve if we do not break the spirit of dependency.

If we believe this is our time to bless the world then let us stop begging for bread and water! Let us trust in Him who is leading us to grant us the wisdom and strength to release the riches in our own nations and neighborhoods.

Political independence has not brought us mental independence. It is all right when a child is dependent. The Apostle Paul said in 1 Cor. 13:11:

"When I was a child, I spake as a child, I understood as a child, I thought as a child: but when I became a man, I put away childish things."

Children speak of only what should be done for them and not what they can also do for others. A child understands that when he has a need, he just has to cry and fuss to have his needs met. A child thinks that the whole world owes him a living. When the child becomes a man, he needs to learn how to put away childish behavior.

Another dimension of this bondage mentality, manifests itself whenever we make efforts to be our own man. What we have come to accept as "blackness" and "Africanness" in a lot of instances is the stereotype that we have been made to accept as "our place." This attitude was developed during the process of slavery and colonialism.

One of the major tools employed was separation and segregation. Therefore, we had areas and facilities whose use were determined on racial basis. There were areas where blacks did not have access to. Even in Africa, where we were colonized in our countries, boundaries were drawn for us concerning which areas we could stay, eat or educate our children.

Over a period of time these physical barriers became mental barriers. You know where to go and where not to go. With the barriers developed the concept of association. You associate the good things with the master's forbidden areas and the cheap and inferior facilities with yourself. Later on, as you settle that disparity as the norm of life, you become comfortable with "your place." As far as you keep to "your place" you are accepted by the master. Many black people have mentally accepted the logic of black is inferior. We may not verbalize it or even be aware of it but it is in our sub-conscious minds.

I have noticed that black people have accepted certain residential areas as being "black" neighborhoods. Certain lifestyles are seen as black and whenever one of us makes the effort to break out of this limitation we think he has become "white", just because he now stays in an area we think is reserved for the former master.

In Africa, I have noticed that on most occasions when people talk about doing something African, they invariably mean doing something cheap and inferior. However, being African has nothing to do with using archaic implements to prepare food and using the same methods some Africans used 400 years ago at their level of development. We have to break these mental barriers to development. We do not have to associate need, lack, inferiority, poverty, shabby accommodation and insufficient education with being black.

The other unfortunate aspect of this syndrome is that when black brothers and sisters get what had been associated with the "master," they start feeling a sense of superiority over their own brethren. That is really sad! It seems as if we are saying "the closer you are to the 'white' man the better you become." Sad!

The lines of demarcation must be broken. This world belongs to God and we have His mandate to have dominion over it.

I run into black brothers who prefer to marry lighter skinned sisters and sisters who think marriage to a light skinned man guarantees romance. I do not mind if you marry a blue, green, red or indigo skinned person so far as it is based on mutual love and not to boost your deflated ego!

It took a process of mis-education to create this condition of dependency and it will take another process of re-education to make us independent of man and only dependent on God who is the real Source of life. I cannot help but recall the words of Job:

"Lo mine eye hath seen all this, mine ear hath heard and understood it. What ye know, the same do I know also: I am not inferior to you."
                                    Job 13:1-2.

See that His eyes are upon you.

Hear what His Spirit is doing in these days.

Understand His purpose for your ethnicity.

Know that He is no respecter of persons...

And ... Break the Myth!

8

Let's Get Ready To Run

It's Time For Us to Run

In Luke 12:54-56 the Bible states:

And he said also to the people, When ye see a cloud rise out of the west, straightway ye say, There cometh a shower; and so it is.

And when ye see the south wind blow, ye say, There will be heat; and it cometh to pass.

Ye hypocrites, ye can discern the face of the sky and of the earth; but how is it that ye do not discern the face of the sky and of the earth; but how is it that ye do not discern this time?

Jesus rebukes people who are not able to discern the times they are living in and calls them hypocrites. It is hypocritical to know the natural signs but not understand the spiritual signs. It is hypocritical to be able to predict the rain and not be able to predict what God is doing. When God works, He never leaves Himself without a witness. He makes His way clear, so that there will be no shadow of doubt as to His plans, purposes and intentions.

It is important to know the times and seasons of God and to realize when your time has come.

There is nothing more tragic than doing the right thing at the wrong time. Sometimes, we get so used to a phase in our lives that we institutionalize that phase and make it a permanent feature in our lives. In other words, what was comfortable to do yesterday becomes comfortable to do forever. Yesterday is for yesterday, today is for today and tomorrow will be for tomorrow. The only person who remains eternal and unchangeable is God Almighty. Apart from Him, man changes in line with the changing of the times and seasons.

We would be drawing an analogy from the Bible in 2nd Samuel 18:19-32 for our edification and to let us know what God is doing in our time.

The background to this story is that David had a son by name of Absalom who had a sister Tamar. This sister was unfortunately raped by one of David's sons who was not of the same mother with Tamar and Absalom. After that incident, Absalom planned to kill his brother. He waited for an opportunity and finally after four years planned a party, invited his brother to be there and killed this brother who had raped his sister. Afterwards, he was banished from Jerusalem.

He later came back and started to plan to take over the throne of David. After sometime he succeeded temporarily to take over the throne of David. He marshalled his forces against his father David, to fight him and to kill him and in the battle that ensued,

Absalom was killed, even though David had given the instruction for him not to be killed. Joab, the chief of the army of David, killed him and when Absalom was killed, it was necessary for the message to be delivered back to David about what had happened at the camp. This recorded incident gives us an indication of the process by which the message was supposed to be sent back to David as we read from 2 Samuel 18:19-32:

> Then said Ahimaaz the son of Zadok, Let me now run, and bear the king tidings, how that the LORD hath avenged him of his enemies.

> And Joab said unto him, Thou shalt not bear tidings this day, but thou shalt bear tidings another day: but this day thou shalt bear no tidings, because the king's son is dead.

> Then said Joab to Cushi, Go tell the king what thou hast seen. And Cushi bowed himself unto Joab, and ran.

> Then said Ahimaaz the son of Zadok yet again to Joab, But howsoever, let me, I pray thee, also run after Cushi. And Joab said, Wherefore wilt thou run, my son, seeing that thou hast no tidings ready?

> But howsoever, said he, let me run. And he said unto him, Run. Then Ahimaaz ran by the way of the plain and overran Cushi.

> And David sat between the two gates: and the watchman went up to the roof over the gate unto the wall, and lifted up his eyes, and looked and behold a man running alone.

> And the watchman cried, and told the king. And the king said, If he be alone, there is tidings in his mouth. And he came apace, and drew near.

> And the watchman saw another man running: and

the watchman called unto the porter, and said, Behold another man running alone. And the king said, He also bringeth tidings.

And the watchman said, Me thinketh the running of the foremost is like the running of Ahimaaz the son of Zadok. And the king said, He is a good man, and cometh with good tidings.

And Ahimaaz called, and said unto the king, All is well. And he fell down to the earth upon his face before the king, and said, Blessed be the LORD thy God, which hath delivered up the men that lifted up their hand against my lord the king.

And the king said, Is the young man Absalom safe? And Ahimaaz answered, When Joab sent the king's servant, and me thy servant, I saw a great tumult, but I knew not what it was.

And the king said unto him, Turn aside, and stand here. And he turned aside, and stood still.

And, behold, Cushi came; and Cushi said, Tidings, my lord the king: for the LORD hath avenged thee this day of all them that rose up against thee.

And the king said unto Cushi, Is the young man Absalom safe? And Cushi answered, The enemies of my lord the king, and all that rise against thee to do thee hurt, be as that young man is.

The Scripture is talking about two people a man called Ahimaaz and another man whom the King James Version calls the "Cushi." In other words the name "Cushi" was not his name but was a description of who he was. He was a Cushite. From our Biblical understanding we know that Cush simply means Ethiopian, and the Cushite refers to the black person or the black individual. Here we see an account of a message to be delivered by a potential of two people -

Ahimaaz and Cush. The Bible says that after victory has been won the normal thing to have been done in this situation was for Ahimaaz to send the message because Ahimaaz was the man who has been sending the message all the time.

As a matter of fact, if you read the same 2nd Samuel 15:36 it states: **"Behold, they have there with them their two sons, Ahimaaz Zadok's son, and Jonathan Abiathar's son; and by them ye shall send unto me every thing that ye can hear."**

In other words, David was giving the instructions that since he was moving out of Jerusalem because of the return of Absalom, any message that was supposed to be sent to him should come through Ahimaaz and another man called Jonathan. So Ahimaaz was the appointed message deliverer to David.

In Chapter 17:17 we read; **"Now Jonathan and Ahimaaz stayed by Enrogel; for they might not be seen to come into the city: and a wench went and told them; and they went and told king David."**

Ahimaaz and Jonathan were set between Jerusalem and the place where David was encamped so if anybody wanted to send a message they will tell Ahimaaz and then he will send it to David.

He was an already established, experienced messenger. So on this occasion when the king had won a great victory, the natural thing was for Ahimaaz to go and deliver the message. Apart from that, Ahimaaz was also the son of a priest called Zadok and also a man of experience. He was a very fast runner. He had been used to that ministry of delivering messages to the king or acting as the king's messenger. However, on this special occasion the times had changed and there was the need for a new order of delivering of messages.

You need to understand that the black people and the Israelites have always been dwelling together. The children of Keturah through Abraham, who were black people, had an inheritance amongst the tribe of Judah. These people have always been dwelling with the Israelites. It is not strange to find black people all throughout the history of Israel; it was not strange that in the army of David there was a Cushite, and when it was time to deliver the message Joab turned to the Cushite and said: "*this is your time.*" "Ahimaaz is experienced but this is your time to go and deliver the message."

Ahimaaz insisted three times to go and deliver the message. The Cushite never asked to deliver the message, he was given the opportunity without asking for it.

The reason why Joab decided not to send Ahimaaz was because this message had to be borne by a man of maturity. Joab knew the two occasions that people with such information had been killed by David. After Saul had died and someone came to report the news, David killed him. The second time another person came to report that Ishbosheth had died, David killed him and so whoever was supposed to carry this new message should know how to carry this message with a measure of caution. He had to carry the message with such tact, wisdom, and maturity and say it in such a way that David would not kill him.

At this point in time, Joab saw the experienced Ahimaaz but he knew he could not take the message. "It is not your time. You have been doing it every time but we need somebody who can handle this message better." When they needed somebody to tell the message with better precision they had to call on the Cushite.

Verse 21 - **"Then said Joab to Cushi, Go tell the king what thou hast seen. And Cushi bowed himself unto Joab, and ran."** I like that. He did not tell the Cushite go and tell the king what he had heard or what he had been told but what he had seen. "Be the original person. You are going to deliver the message which is original to you. You are not going to tell a message which is a duplication of what you have heard before but you have to take the responsibility of reporting the things that have been shown to you."

I believe that the Spirit of God is calling on the Cushites of this era, that it is time to deliver the message concerning the things that we have seen, that have been taught us personally, uniquely, originally and individually. I believe that the time of duplicating messages which we have read from others is over.

It is time for the Cushite to deliver the message which he himself has tasted of. There was a time when every message we delivered was a message that had been reported to us. We quoted what had been, but the time has come when the Cushite should hear from God himself. The time has come when the Cushite does not have to look up to somebody for credibility. The time has come when the Cushite must tell the message which does not have to be validated by a "white" man

For most of us, we think something is true because a white man has confirmed it. We do not need the confirmation of any man to our message. The only person who needs to confirm our message is God Almighty!

When I travel to the nations, I do not go to give them what they have given to me. I give them what God has given me.

Let us tell the nations what we have seen. Have you seen anything? Has God shown you anything? Has God taught you anything? Then tell the nations about it!! *Yes I can Tell the world about this I can tell the nations I'm blessed. etc*

The Cushite took the message and started running with that message. While he was running, this man who had always been doing the job - Ahimaaz said, "give me the chance." Joab said, "your time is not now you do not have any message and you cannot run without a message," but he said, "whether I have a message or not let me run." Joab said "you are not ready." Ahimaaz replied," whether I am ready or not, I want to run."

When people's times are past, they still want to run. Ahimaaz will run although he has no message. He will still move. He will still use his experience. When Ahimaaz started running the Bible says, he outran the Cushite because he was a fast runner.

He had the technology. He had the infrastructure, so he was faster, although he had no message. The Bible says he ran faster because he ran in the plain. He ran in the cool area.

The Cushite, on the contrary, was running through the hard, rocky areas because he did not know the short cut. He had to go through the long process. He was running through the thorny areas, through the poverty deprivation, malnourished areas but he was running. He was running because he had been sent to run.

The Bible says how lovely are the feet of those who carry the good news. He had lovely feet but he pierced his feet, wounded his feet because he was running in the terrain he was not accustomed to. He was running in a situation that he was not familiar with, but he had to run because he had been given a message. The Bible says Ahimaaz was spotted from afar off - David said "surely if it is Ahimaaz and he is running alone then he must have a message.

Men with a message sometimes have to run alone. Men who always need to run in company may lose their message because they need the company of other peoples opinion in order to move. When he arrived David asked:

"What did you see?" He replied: "Well, there is good news for the king. Your enemies have been defeated."

David then asked: "What happened to Absalom?"

Ahimaaz responded: "I did not see anything. When Joab sent me I saw people gather, but I did not see what they were looking at. I just saw them and that is all."

He did not have any message. He was not a first hand witness. David said to him: "Stand aside." When you run without a message you will be told to stand aside. No matter how fast you run, brothers and sisters, you have to have something in your mouth.

If you have nothing in your mouth and you run as fast as possible, when you get there and you are asked what message you have, you will start scratching your head. People who run without messages always are sidelined. It does not matter how far you travel, how many times you travel, if you do not have any message you will be told to stand aside. The important thing is not whether you go but what is in your mouth.

It's A New Day!

I am not keen on running unless I have something to say. When you have something to say, the running gives you substance. God is telling Ahimaaz to stand aside because he had run before but this time "he doesn't have a message."

The Lord is telling Ahimaaz "you do not have any message." Ahimaaz will fight. It is difficult to stand aside because he is used to running. Gone are the days when all of Africa would just sit down and organize one big crusade for one white man to come and turn all our pastors into ushers and counselors; the days when we would pack our Bibles and go to a conference somewhere and listen to a white man lecture us on how to win Africa when he had not been to Africa before, are over! *God is saying stand aside Ahimaaz.* You did it yesterday but today, stand aside because there is a new hour, a new day and a new man must deliver the message. *This is our time to reach our own.*

When your time comes you must know how to run with the message. There is time for everything. There is time for babies to be men and there is time for men to be old men. When you are an old man, your baby takes care of you because he is now the man. Sometime ago, some people came to give us the message of the Gospel they preached to us. They taught us the ways of God. Now they have also become old men!

I believe that God is prophetically speaking to the modern day Cushite not to be intimidated by the fast running of Ahimaaz. God is telling the modern day Cushite, *"you may not have the money and all the technology that the people have but I have given you a message. You must know that I have put something inside you that must be told to the nations of the world."*

Sometimes when God calls you, it is very easy to look to the people who have been running all along and question God; "But they did it yesterday;" when God will be telling you it is your time. When it is your time to tell the message, although you have not run before, you must learn how to run. You may run slowly, make some mistakes, go through thorny places but you have to run. It is time to run and when our time comes to run, there should be no excuse.

We cannot complain that we do not have money because when your time comes to run you do not need to complain, you just exercise your feet. If you do not run, no message will be delivered, because the people you are trusting to run and deliver the message do not have any message.

God is telling the black people all over the world that their time has come. The time of servanthood and slavery of the black man has come to an end. For so many years we have been in bondage, but that time has come to an end. The last system that needs to be broken will be broken in South Africa, and when that is done, it will signify the completeness of the time of slavery of black people all over the world and usher in the time for their lifting up, because God has a process of making leaders. He makes leaders by first making them servants.

God does not raise leaders who have never served. He makes you a servant and then you become a leader. Before God chose Israel to be a nation among nations they had to serve for four hundred years. They had to be servants and then after that God said "*I will make you a special people.*"

We have to discern the times. The clock is ticking, the times are changing. We need to recognize this and we need to bear the responsibility that comes with that understanding, because until we are able to bear the responsibility, our time will pass us by.

I fear to think of our time passing us by; that our suffering has been in vain, that we have suffered so long, like the people of Israel who were in Egypt. They suffered so long in the wilderness and when the time of deliverance came, they died in the wilderness because they did not discern the time. All they needed to do was to change their slave mentality and start to think differently, but they could not because they had been taught to think as slaves.

When it is your time to run you have to run. When it is your time to speak you have to speak. When it is your time to launch out, you have to launch out because that is the only time you have. If you miss it that is the end. It is like buying a rain coat in the rainy season and packing it in your wardrobe. If you fail to wear it in the rainy season you cannot wear it in the hot weather. When it is the rainy season and you have your rain coat, wear it! There is nothing permanent. God's spotlight keeps moving, it stays on you to do what you are supposed to do, then to another, until they do what they are supposed to do and it keeps moving. It will not stay on you forever. It stays on you for a time and for a purpose. When the light is on you and God says now you run and tell my message, you have to run in all the power He has given to you.

We need to understand what the Spirit of God is saying in this hour. When it is your time to run you may arrive late but you will have the word. God is not just interested in how fast you run, He is interested in what message you are running with.
In Romans 9:15 & 16, the Bible says:

For he saith to Moses, I will have mercy on whom I will have mercy, and I will have compassion on whom I will have compassion.

So then it is not of him that willeth, nor of him that runneth, but of God that showeth mercy.

The Bible says the race is not for the swift, it is not for the man who has a church and has all the nice furnishings, the race is not for the person who is bold, but the race is for the person who has received the mercy of God at a point in time. That is why you do not need to be intimidated because you see someone running faster than you, because he had better gadgets to run faster than you.

Businessmen, lawyers, inventors, teachers, your time has come, young people, your time has come. You may be starting late but you must run with purpose. You are starting late but the important thing is that God has shown mercy on you at this time. You are starting late but you have the favor of God. I believe we have what it takes. I know that we do not have the best of everything. Our neighborhoods are deprived economically because of circumstances within our control which we did **not** control. We have messed up some good opportunities and we are suffering for it, but I hope we will learn our lessons.

You do not let the past stop you and so put your head between your two legs and start crying that God has not given you anything. You may not have the legs but you have a message.

In these times, I believe God is going to raise giants. I do not know how He is going to do it. It is going to be a miracle. The only way we can do the things we want is through miracles. The day we stop trusting God for miracles we are doomed. We do not move by the economy.

God promises, "*I will cause rivers of living water to break forth in the wilderness for you.*" We do not move because there is a change in government legislation. Our hope is not in a democratic rule. We have to believe in the supernatural and God taking us up by miracles. If God does not carry us we are stuck where we are. It is the miracles of God that will save us, and we have to live in the miraculous. We have to trust God to do beyond what our natural ability can do because we are years behind the world.

When I tell you that God has put his finger on us at this time, it is prophetically right. We need to know our history so we can know our future. We have to move backwards in order to move forwards. When we want to trace black history, we do not trace it in a narrow cultural sense. We have to go backward and see how God has dealt with us in difficult times.

Whenever the world has been in a crisis the black man has always appeared on the scene. After the flood, when the world needed a leader, He called Nimrod the son of Cush. When Moses was taken out of Pharaoh's camp, it took a black man, Jethro to teach him the ways of God. When the people of Israel were going to the promised land it took a black man, Hobab to direct them to the promised land. They have always been around. God has always relied on these black people in times of crises.

When it was a time of crisis and nobody could speak to David, it took a black man to take the message to him. He knew how to take the message. He had the wisdom to tackle the problem. When Jeremiah the prophet was put into a dungeon, and Israel was in a crisis, it took an Ethiopian eunuch to set him free.

When it was time for Paul to be sent to the mission field it took black men to lay hands on him and send him out. When Jesus was going to the cross it took a black man to carry the cross.

Even though Nimrod messed up God's plan with selfish ambition, in this new restoration, we must be careful to give God all the Glory. Thank God for Jesus. He sets us free, He liberates our mind.

The Liberator is Jesus the Son of the Living God and when you come to Him, He does not just liberate your spirit, He also liberates your mind and your thinking.

He re-defines your history and puts you on a winning path. We need Jesus to liberate us because He is the connection to our true history!

It was long before creation
That God predestined that you should be Black
So there would be none, in the whole world like you,
Filled with His Glory, Honor and Power
You are Blessed Africa.

Yes the Gold, The diamond and more
Of those precious stones He put them in you
so there will be no place, in the whole world like you
Filled with His Blessing, Wealth and His Glory
You are Blessed Africa.

Africa rise, for God has Blessed you,
His Glory is shining all over you,
Reach out and touch the whole world with Jesus.
He filled you with Power to turn it around.

Song by Emmanuel Owusu-Sekyere

About the Author

Dr. Mensa Otabil pastors the six thousand member International Central Gospel Church, established in 1984 in Accra, Ghana, on the West Coast of Africa. He functions as a pastor's pastor to many men and women in Christian ministry who continue to draw on his wisdom and maturity in the things of God. He also ministers in conferences and seminars in several countries where his down-to-earth rendering of profound truths have impacted many lives.

Pastor Otabil holds two honorary doctorate degrees in Humanities and Divinity. He lives with his wife, Joy and their daughters, Sompa and Nhyira, and son, Yoofi, in the city of Accra.

Send all comments and inquiries to:

Mr. Mensa Otabil,
International Central Gospel Church,
P. O. Box 7933,
Accra-North, Ghana

OR

Dr. Mensa Otabil
c/o
Pneuma Life Publishing
P.O. Box 10612
Bakersfield, CA 93389

Beyond the Rivers of Ethiopia $6.95

Beyond the Rivers of Ethiopia is a powerful and revealing look into God's purpose for the Black Race. It gives scholastic yet simple answers to questions you have always had about the Black presence in the Bible. At the heart of this book is a challenge and call to the offspring of the Children of Africa both on the continent and throughout the world to come to grips with their true identity as they go Beyond the Rivers of Ethiopia.

OTHER BOOKS BY Dr. Mensa Otabil:

Four Laws of Productivity $7.95

In Genesis 1:28, God commanded man to do four things: (1) "Be fruitful, and (2) multiply, and (3) replenish the earth, and (4) subdue it: and have dominion .." In the past, many people read and thought that this scripture only meant to have many children. This scriptural passage is not confined to reproduction, but is the foundation for all productivity. The Four Laws of Productivity by Dr. Mensa Otabil will show you how to: Discover God's gift in you, develop the gift, and how to be truly productive in life. The principles revealed in this timely book will radically change your life.

BOOKS BY Dr. Myles Munroe:

Becoming A Leader	**$9.95**
Becoming A Leader Workbook	**$7.95**
How to Transform Your Ideas into Reality	**$7.95**
Single, Married, Separated and Life After Divorce	**$7.95**
Understanding Your Potential	**$7.95**
Understanding Your Potential Workbook	**$5.95**
Releasing Your Potential	**$7.95**
Releasing Your Potential	**$5.95**
The Pursuit of Purpose	**$7.95**

Beyond the Rivers of Ethiopia $6.95

Beyond the Rivers of Ethiopia is a powerful and revealing look into God's purpose for the Black Race. It gives scholastic yet simple answers to questions you have always had about the Black presence in the Bible. At the heart of this book is a challenge and call to the offspring of the Children of Africa both on the continent and throughout the world to come to grips with their true identity as they go Beyond the Rivers of Ethiopia.

OTHER BOOKS BY Dr. Mensa Otabil:

Four Laws of Productivity $7.95

Success has no favorites. But it does have associates. Success will come to anyone who will pay the price to receive its benefits. *Four Laws of Productivity* will give you four powerful keys that will help you achieve your life's goals. *Four Laws of Productivity* by Dr. Mensa Otabil will show you how to: Discover God's gift in you, develop your gift, perfect your gift, and utilized your gift to its maximun potential. The principles revealed in this timely book will radically change your life.

BOOKS BY Dr. Myles Munroe:

Becoming A Leader	**$9.95**
Becoming A Leader Workbook	**$7.95**
How to Transform Your Ideas into Reality	**$7.95**
Single, Married, Separated and Life After Divorce	**$7.95**
Understanding Your Potential	**$7.95**
Understanding Your Potential Workbook	**$5.95**
Releasing Your Potential	**$7.95**
Releasing Your Potential Workbook	**$5.95**
The Pursuit of Purpose	**$7.95**

Strategies for Saving the Next Generation   **$4.95**
by Dave Burrows

Talk to Me *by Dave Burrows*   **$5.95**

Mobilizing Human Resources *by Richard Pinder*   **$5.95**

The Minister's Topical Bible $14.95
by Derwin Stewart

The Minister's Topical Bible covers every aspect of the ministry providing quick and easy access to scriptures in a variety of ministry related topics. This handy reference tool can be effectively used in leadership training, counseling, teaching, sermon preparation and personal study.

Exciting cassette tapes by Dr. Mensa Otabil

Rising of a New Generation $6.00
Raising a Powerful Generation $6.00
Fruit of the Spirit - 2 tapes $10.00
Fret Not $6.00
Something Out of Nothing $6.00
Increasing in the Kingdom of God $6.00
The Presence/ Power of God to Heal $6.00
The Basis of Correct Prayer $6.00
The Kingdom of God in Our Lives $6.00
How to Study the Bible $6.00
Principles That Govern our Prayers $6.00
The Work of Your Hands $6.00
Rediscovering Work and Industry $6.00
Fresh Wells of Water $6.00
A Life of Fruitfulness $6.00
The Principles of Dominion 2 Tapes $12.00
Righteousness Exalts 2 Tapes $12.00
Hold the Dream 2 Tapes $12.00
The Blessing of Abraham 2 Tapes $12.00
Power at Work in Us $6.00
The Lord Has Need of You $6.00
Don't Run from the Battle $6.00
Run to Obtain $6.00
No Condemnation The Chastisement
     of the Lord $6.00